Markets
of
Provence

Markets
of
Provence

A CULINARY TOUR OF SOUTHERN FRANCE

Foreword by
PATRICIA WELLS

Text by Dixon Long
Recipes by Ruthanne Long
Photographs by David Wakely

CollinsPublishersSanFrancisco
A Division of HarperCollinsPublishers

It takes many people to make a book, and many more to make it the best it can be. We are grateful to Jenny Barry, Maura Carey Damacion, Meesha Halm, Lynne Noone, Carole Vandermeyde, and others at HarperCollins for believing in this project and giving us their trust and guidance; to our editor, Carolyn Miller, for her insight, humor, patience, and careful attention to detail; to Connie Barney, whose expertise enhanced the recipes; to Patricia Wells for the glass of wine at her mountaintop home, her inspiration, and a beautiful foreword. We salute Joan Olson, our compositor, and Marlene McLoughlin, for the cover border and the map. Thanks also to Mark Woodworth and Mark Rhynsburger for their careful proofreading.

There are many others to thank for their support, including our families and friends. To name only a few: Hazel White—a special friend in the making of this book, Jessie Bunn, Roberta Cairney, Zippie Collins, Marjorie and Lancelot Farrar, Tove and Jorge Fenger, Jack Hagstrom, Genevieve and Michel Laverne, Diana Lorentz, Linda Lorentz, Dayna Macy, Ida Martin, Jim McNulty, Claudie Pons-Renouf, Velia and Bob Pryce, Beth Roy, Zhdan Rudnyckyj, Ward Schumacker, Pamela Sheldon-Johns, Gordon Smith, Françoise and Jean Spati, Michele Sudduth, Charlotte Turgeon, Elizabeth and Mark Wholey, and Alison Zetterquist. Finally, our thanks to Anne Dickerson, who brought the four of us together and encouraged us throughout.

We cannot forget the faces of the many farmers and vendors we met and who shared with us their knowledge of how to bring the freshest, ripest, most appealing produce to the market. To those and others who opened their doors and stalls to us, *merci mille fois!*

—S.S., D.L., R.L., D.W.

This book is dedicated to the hardworking farmers and vendors of Provence. We hope it will contribute to the continued life of the open markets in Provence and around the world.

First published 1996 by Collins Publishers San Francisco
1160 Battery Street, San Francisco, California 94111

HarperCollins Web Site: http://www.harpercollins.com

© Sharon Smith, David Wakely, Dixon and Ruthanne Long
Text and recipes © Dixon and Ruthanne Long
Photographs © David Wakely
Foreword © Patricia Wells
All rights reserved, including the right of reproduction in whole or in part in any form.

HarperCollins®, 📖 ® and CollinsPublishersSanFrancisco™
are trademarks of HarperCollinsPublishers Inc.

Printed in Hong Kong
10 9 8 7 6 5 4 3 2 1

Library of Congress Cataloging-in-Publication Data
Long, Dixon.
   Markets of Provence: a culinary tour of southern France / text by Dixon Long and recipes by Ruthanne Long; photographs by David Wakely; foreword by Patricia Wells.
      p.   cm.
   Includes index.
   ISBN 0-00-225061-6
   1. Cookery, French—Provençal style.   2. Cookery—France—Provence.
   3. Farmers' markets—France—Provence.   4. Provence—Social life and customs.
   5. Provence—Description and travel.   I. Long, Ruthanne.   II. Title.
TX719.2.P75L66   1996
641.59449—dc20
                                      95-42042

Book and cover design: Sharon Smith
Editing: Carolyn Miller
Composition: Joan Olson
Recipe consultant: Connie Barney
Watercolor cover border and map:
   Marlene McLoughlin

A Smith/Wakely Production

The illustration on page 89 was taken from *Des Hommes, Des Murs et Des Abeilles*, published by Musée de Salon and de la Crau, Salon-de-Provence (1993).

CONTENTS

FOREWORD

by Patricia Wells

Each Tuesday morning I awake with a childlike sense of eager anticipation. Not just any day, but market day in Provence! Almost better than Christmas, or a birthday or anniversary, market day clocks the change of the seasons, the mood of our village, the spirit of the times. And so it has been, for hundreds of years, for all those who came before me in the Provençal town of Vaison-la-Romaine.

By five in the morning, independent merchants are already packing up their vans, trucks, rolling paella pushcarts, and customized pizza wagons, ready to begin their drive to this old Roman town. By eight, they have gathered in the Place Montfort, where a *placeur* assigns them a cherished space. Soon they will scatter all over town, setting up shop along La Grand Rue, in front of the post office, beside the ruins, trailing, meandering, weaving through the village, ready for the steady flow of customers who begin to arrive a little before nine.

Within moments, the town is transformed, filled with the heady fragrance of herbal soaps: lemon verbena, lime, old rose, honeysuckle, lavender, and honey. The welcome scent of local herbs leaps from the orderly baskets of a dozen variously seasoned olives, flecked with preserved lemons, fronds of fresh dill, bunches of wild thyme, sprinklings of hot pepper, spicy oil, fennel seeds, crushed cumin. And as the coffee woman from Montelimar begins roasting a batch of plump Maragogype beans, it's as though the caffeine in the air gives us all an extra boost of energy.

Musicians begin to warm up: There's Philippe, *chanteur des rues,* with his Barbary organ, and the Peruvian band with their colorful costumes and energetic, reedy voices. Soon all those wicker baskets and string bags will be bulging with first-of-season tomatoes, blushing orange apricots, pots of tiny-leafed basil, strings of plump garlic, containers of diminutive telline clams, and miniature disks of fragile white goat cheese.

And so the scene is repeated throughout Provence, day in, day out, year after year, decade after decade, in the sun, rain, and snow, and even on holidays. Like a giant traveling carnival, with the cast of characters changing from village to village, market day is a spectacle that has survived almost untouched by modern times.

In Provence, you don't need a cookbook. Just stand around long enough and you'll gather the local recipe for *pistou* (always fresh white beans and cranberry beans, lots of carrots, and never turnips in this traditional bean and vegetable soup), for the fishmonger's whole bonito studded with anchovies, for the butcher's guinea hen roasted with black olives from Nyons, for the farmer's artichokes braised in garlic and white wine.

Want to know if the moon is right for planting onions? Ask Monsieur Raynaud. If the moon is waning, it's time to plant vegetables that grow beneath the earth. (But don't make your *confiture* now, or the sugar will rise to the surface!)

There's almost nothing you can't buy on market day. Custom-made leather sandals, olive-wood salad bowls,

Opinel knives in more than a dozen sizes. Plants and seeds, Moroccan spices, organic grains, live chickens, herbs for eating and herbs for healing, fantasy beeswax candles, gingerbread cakes, deep-fried potato balls, wild boar sausages, Provençal tablecloths, fresh ears of corn.

At the market you can meet old friends and stop for a cup of espresso at the Sporting Bar. You may run into the plumber you've been trying to reach for days, and soon the faucet will drip no more.

Over time, you may notice that people resemble their wares. The fat man selling a sack of plump roasted peanuts in the shell looks as though he's consumed quite a few peanuts in his day. The asparagus woman is tiny and thin as a stalk. The wrinkles on the wizened old couple selling overgrown carrots covered with dirt imitate those of their sturdy root vegetables. The goat cheese woman is demure and immaculate, just like her fresh, delicate cheese.

At the edge of town, the small independent farmers—*paysans*—arrive with their paltry but venerable crops. Ask for two dozen eggs and the farmwife replies: "I only have six eggs, but they're big, and my chickens are very healthy." Colorful yellow zucchini blossoms sell for ten francs a dozen, but the farmer offers thirteen. "Are you superstitious?" he asks. "No," I respond. "Well, I am," he laughs, handing me fourteen freshly picked blossoms.

My baskets are bulging and my coin purse is empty—it's time to return home and begin the day's feast. Thirteen for dinner tonight. On the menu, home-cured black olives from our handful of olive trees; zucchini blossoms deep-fried in curry batter; Provençal *pistou*; sourdough bread flecked with linseed and sesame; and apricot-almond tart for dessert. The *cigales* are singing, the bread oven is fired up, and all's right with the world.

INTRODUCTION

Somewhere in Provence, every morning of the week, in every kind of weather, small farmers and market gardeners get up before dawn to drive their *camionnettes* to a village. They maneuver into narrow streets and squares, set up simple trestle tables, and unload boxes of fruit and vegetables harvested only hours before at the peak of ripeness. On good days—and most days are good—the Provençal sun transforms ripe peppers to fire, honey to melted gold, and olives into baroque jewels. Eggplants, tomatoes, and cherries glisten, melons send messages to your nose, and everything asks to be tasted.

There are many other things to see and to buy, but most people come here for the food: vegetables, fish, eggs and poultry, salad greens. And the cheeses—what a feast! They're made from the milk of cows, goats, and sheep. Some are hard, some soft. There are old favorites like Brie and *bleu*. We always need Parmesan for our pasta, and, of course, a wedge of *tomme* or Cantal to nibble on. There are ranks and files of fresh white goat cheese, some powdered with ash or wrapped in chestnut leaves. Each is displayed like a precious object in a museum case.

Markets of Provence was written to share our passion for these open markets. Anyone planning to visit Provence will find that focusing on the markets is a good way to experience the region. We've chosen a different one for each day of the week. There's tiny Bonnieux, a village of a few hundred people at the top of a mountain. At the other end of the scale is Aix-en-Provence, a city of several hundred thousand. Its elegant market has enough different lettuces to please a royal palate, and seafood straight from the docks at Marseilles. These are only a sampling; at the end of each chapter we've listed many more weekly markets that may fit your itinerary.

We also show you what shoppers look for in a little farmer's market like Sénas, where local people bring produce just picked from their gardens. We share our ideas about cooking at home and eating out, and evoke something of daily life in this part of southern France. We introduce you to people like Linda Lorentz, who makes and sells goat cheese, and Jean Spati, who hunts truffles. We provide recipes using regional food in ways you can re-create in your own homes with local supplies.

Every chapter has sections on special foods, such as goat cheese, honey, and *herbes de Provence*. In the "Resources" section at the end of the book, you'll find lists in French and English of the produce in the markets, and locations and telephone numbers of restaurants and places of interest. We also include a conversion chart to help with shopping and cooking, and even some useful French phrases to try in the markets.

Markets have existed for centuries, but the cornucopia that is the open market today was not always so bountiful. Flood, drought, and poverty were the defining aspects of life in Provence for generations. With the establishment of the Fifth Republic in 1958, large-scale irrigation and flood-control projects were begun, and finally completed in the early 1980s. The forgotten people of the Vaucluse and the Bouches-du-Rhône began to experience the benefits. They expanded their gardens and orchards, leading Provence to become the fruit and vegetable basket for France and Europe.

The love of good eating is central to French culture. Compared to our American world of fast foods and supermarket sameness, the outdoor markets of Provence are an expression of a different style of living. They hew to traditional values of quality, freshness, and presentation, operating in ways that have not changed materially for centuries. In an important sense, the open markets stand for continuity against the tumult of change in contemporary life.

There are no secrets to shopping in the open markets. It helps to speak some French, but we learned most of what we know by keeping our eyes open. When we buy vegetables, we look for the word *pays,* which means "local," on the small chalkboards or bits of cardboard stuck in the corners of the boxes. Otherwise, the vegetables are marked with the region or country of origin. Everything is sold by metric weight, so we have rough equivalents in mind to make conversions. If we're uncertain how much we want, we say *"Deux grandes poignées, ça suffira"* ("Two big handfuls, that'll be enough"). Nearly every vendor has a battery-powered scale, but adding machines aren't common, so there's still a lot of pencil pushing. A scrap of paper with the total goes in the bag with the purchase. Vendors are scrupulously honest. If the numbers are confusing, hold out a handful of coins and they'll take what's owed.

Markets start around eight o'clock. During the morning a fellow dressed like a policeman collects money from each vendor: stall rent, usually about five francs for each running meter. By eleven, most shoppers have started home with full baskets. At noon, sellers pack their unsold produce, fold their tables, and sweep their spaces. Then they're off for lunch with family and friends. Surely there will be a cold bottle of the local *vin rosé* on the table, along with many of the same good things we've been buying.

The supermarket has invaded France, not only the big towns but some of the villages. People patronize it because they can save money and find items the weekly markets don't carry. But in the end, nothing replaces the open market, the vitality and enthusiasm of buyers and sellers, and the pleasure of doing business in this uncomplicated way. Nowhere else is the food so genuinely fresh from the earth and the hand that harvested it. Nowhere else do the wide blue sky, the blazing sun, and the gusting mistral attend the act of marketing—not shopping, but marketing—raising it from a humble necessity to a high art.

• Vaison·la·Romaine

• Séguret

• Orange

• Beaumes·de·Venise

Châteauneuf·du·Pape

• Carpentras

DENTELLES DE MONTMIRAIL

MONT VENTOUX

0 938

SORGUE

0 942

Pont·du·Gard

D 981

N 100

• AVIGNON

N 100

D 973

0 936

l'ISLE sur la SORGUE

Gordes

Rousillon

Coustellet

Goult

Cavaillon

Oppède·le·Vieux

BONNIEUX

Fort·de·Buoux

APT

Saignon

Saint·Martin·de·Castillon

Céreste

CALAVO

N 100

GRAND LUBERON

Cucuron

Lourmarin

PETIT LUBERON

CADENET

la·TOUR·d'AIGUES

D 973

VER

Villelaure

Pertuis

Châteaurenard

Beaucaire

Tarascon

SAINT·RÉMY·de·PROVENCE

CHAÎNE DES

les Baux

Paradou • Maussane·les·Alpilles

ALPILLES

ARLES

Sénas

Salon·de·Provence

DURANCE

AT

LUBERON

Montagne·Sainte·Victoir

AUTOROUTE DU SOLEIL

PROVENCE

CAMARGUE

ÉTANG

DE

BERRE

AIX·en·PROVENCE

Marignane
Airport

• MARSEILLE

MER MÉDITERRANÉE

RHONE

AT

Forcalquier •

• Viens

FRANCE

PARIS

BELG LUX GERMA

ATLANTIC OCEAN

SWIT

IT

PROVENCE

SPAIN

MÉDITERRANÉ

THE MARKETS

MONDAY IN CADENET
A Gateway Town

When you cross the Durance River heading north on Route D943, you'll see the town of Cadenet clambering up the side of a distant hill. It's a dazzling sight in the late afternoon, when the sun strikes the town from the west, highlighting its golden color and emphasizing its pyramidal form. At the top of the pyramid is a crown of pine trees. As you come closer, you'll spy the ruins of a stone wall just below them: the remains of a château, now partially restored as a splendid site for concerts and outdoor events.

Cadenet has some thirty-two hundred inhabitants: farmers, commuters who work in or near Aix-en-Provence, local tradesmen, and a few expatriates from northern Europe and North America. For more than two thousand years, Cadenet was in the path of conquerors. The first of these were the Romans, who entered Provence

Facing page: The bounty from a day at the market. *Above:* Cadenet's main shopping street, always lively, is even more so on market day.

3

from the southeast, moved across the plains of the Pays d'Aigues, or south Luberon, through the narrow pass cut by the waters of the Aigue Brun and thence into the Pays d'Apt, or north Luberon. The modern town was founded rather recently, in A.D. 877.

In the late eighteenth century, Cadenet became a center for the production of wicker baskets, made from the branches of willows that grew along the banks of the Durance and on small islands in the river. The old Provençal word for wicker, *cade,* probably gave the town its name. In 1988, a basket museum was built where the basket makers once worked. A videotape and a small collection of photographs document the site, and show what the workers looked like. It's fascinating to compare the faces in these old daguerreotypes with the faces you see in the markets today. Clothes and hairstyles may change, but physiognomy endures.

We never feel properly prepared if we enter a market without a basket in our hands. It protects vegetables from being bruised, and is easier to manage than a handful of sacks. It may be a traditional wicker one, or a colorful fiber basket from Morocco or Tunisia.

Right: The rooftops of Cadenet, seen from the ruined ramparts of the château. *Facing page, top:* Monsieur Turcan cuts a tablecloth from fabric as bright as the Provençal sun. *Facing page, bottom:* Looking, touching, and smelling are all part of the art of marketing.

If you don't have a basket when you first arrive in the market, you may want to look for the basket seller right away and equip yourself. If you'd rather not bother, you can get along with the ubiquitous plastic sacks that almost every vendor offers.

Cadenet is a practical working town of the Luberon, large enough to house the regional tax offices but too small for a supermarket. Its narrow alleys and back streets are as charming as those of any postcard village, while its commercial streets, full of parked vehicles and whizzing motorcycles, are quite ordinary. The *maison de la presse* (the newspaper and magazine store) in the center of the village is an excellent source of guidebooks and pamphlets about the region, along with novels, poetry, and reminiscences of local writers. It also has a well-stocked magazine rack and, for those who come early in the morning, a selection of foreign newspapers.

The Monday-morning market in Cadenet is popular because it offers a chance to lay in staples for the week ahead. There are also three good bakers in town, and a branch of the Crédit Agricole where many residents bank, so a number of weekly chores can be combined in one visit. This goes along with some gossiping in the streets or at one of the cafés and, for some, participation in a game of *boules* (also called *pétanque*), a kind of horseshoe pitching

(continued on page 8)

Facing page: It takes a day or more to make baskets the old-fashioned way. *Top:* This couple makes their handsome baskets at home in Toulouse and sells them in the market. *Above:* Colorful soft baskets from Morocco.

BASKET MAKING IN CADENET

Until quite recently—a decade or so after the end of World War II—baskets woven of willow branches from local river banks were the predominant means of bringing the morning's purchases home from market. Change comes slowly to Provence, but the impact of cheap imports and new materials ultimately destroyed the domestic basket industry. You can still see a few of the big, deep, square-handled shopping baskets in the local markets, almost always on the arms of older women. Young people will more often be seen clutching a handful of plastic sacks, one from each of the vendors with whom they've shopped.

Cadenet has a fine small basketry museum on the Avenue Philippe de Girard, next door to the tax office. It exhibits many of the articles produced by basket makers who worked in an atelier on the same site. The collection is divided into four sections: home, work, childhood, and travel. This diversity illustrates the central place wickerwork had in everyday life as late as the early 1900s, when more than three hundred basket makers (mostly women) worked in the village. There were wicker household articles (chairs, trunks, food containers, strollers) and tools for use in the home and garden (bread-rising baskets, bird traps, wine-bottle holders, sewing baskets). Hunters and fishermen, then as now, had special baskets to put their catch in. Farmers had different baskets for harvesting cherries, grapes, olives, and strawberries. Dogs and cats had baskets to sleep in, ducks and chickens to lay eggs in. Baskets served as bird feeders. There were specially shaped baskets for serving asparagus, bread, fruit, cheese, and berries. Women used baskets to store make-up and as handbags. Have we neglected to mention anything? Ah, yes—a basket in which freshly ironed linen was laid.

After World War I, the production of baskets continued, using materials imported from other parts of France and, up until World War II, from Malaysia. The last workshop closed in 1978, when foreign competition and plastics finally put an end to the industry. If your French is up to it, the museum will show a short videotape of an interview with a woman who worked all her life in a basket factory.

(continued from page 5)

with steel balls, that takes place daily in front of the Bar du Jeu de Boules, behind the church. Inside this church is a carved stone baptismal font bearing the earliest known representation of grapevines in Provence.

The market is centered on the Place du Tambour d'Arcole, where on market day you'll find a key maker and a typical mélange of clothing, hardware, honey, soap, flower, and vegetable sellers. You'll also see a statue of the drummer boy from Cadenet, André Estienne, frozen in a triumphant pose. When Republican armies led by Bonaparte were rallying against the Austrians in 1796, this brave lad swam a river and fooled the enemy into thinking that his drumbeats were the guns of attackers. For this and other acts of courage, André was awarded the Legion of Honor at the age of twenty-six, and after his death his name was inscribed in the Panthéon in Paris.

As you move past André's statue, you'll be greeted by mouthwatering aromas from the poultry seller's open rotisserie. To the right of the glass case where plucked birds are displayed stands a vertical gas-fired engine with four parallel rows of spits. Five or more birds are turning on each spit, their juices cascading from top to bottom. The *patron,* known locally as Jean d'Oeuf (or John Egg—a Danish transplant, as you can tell by his hair

and eyes) or one of his family slides the roasted birds off the spit as they're ready and pops them into foil-lined bags for clients who have ordered ahead and gone on to finish their marketing.

Shopping for poultry is complicated in France, because male, female, young, and old birds are named and cooked differently (see "A Market Glossary," page 122). If you don't want a whole bird you can buy parts, with or without giblets. Beside the chickens are trays of tiny headless quail with their legs trussed up and their wings tucked underneath them. Then come the ducks, pigeons, rab-

Facing page: The proud and triumphant drummer boy is the centerpiece of the Cadenet market. *Below:* Bags and braids of white and purple garlic, enough for the whole village.

bits, and sometimes a turkey or two. Depending on the season, partridges are also available.

The locations of market vendors are determined by custom and seniority, and remain the same year after year. At harvest time in June, you'll find the garlic seller in the Place du Tambour, in front of Allemand's hardware store. She has both mild white garlic and the stronger purple variety. You can buy individual heads, or a braid (the French word is *tresse*) to hang up for handy plucking. In the spring, she'll have green garlic, tender young bulbs with stalks that are wonderful in potato soup. Here too are sellers of seedling herbs and a selection of small annuals to enhance the garden.

To the left from the Place du Tambour is the main shopping street

Green Garlic Soup
SOUPE À L'AIL FRAIS

Farmers plant garlic at the winter solstice and harvest it at the summer solstice. In April we begin to see young garlic stalks in the markets, soon followed by small, tender fava beans. This quickly prepared soup can be served hot or cold. SERVES 4.

4   cups chicken stock
1   to 14 stalks green garlic, cut into ½-inch pieces
1   large baking potato, peeled and chopped
1   teaspoon *herbes de Provence*
½   bay leaf
Scant ¼ teaspoon salt
1½ pounds young fava beans in the pod, shelled and blanched for 1 minute
¼   cup heavy cream
Freshly ground black pepper to taste
Chopped fresh chives (optional)

Put the chicken stock in a 2-quart saucepan. Add the garlic, potatoes, herbs, and salt. Simmer over medium heat until the vegetables are fork tender, about 15 to 20 minutes. Remove the bay leaf.

Place the mixture in a blender or food processor fitted with the metal blade and process to a medium-coarse puree, or use a food mill with the medium disk.

Return the mixture to the saucepan and add the fava beans, heavy cream, and freshly ground black pepper. Bring the soup to a simmer. Ladle into bowls and garnish with chives, if desired.

in Cadenet. About two blocks long, this narrow, sloping street has a medieval feeling about it. Three-story buildings crowd in on both sides, with shops below and living spaces above. Halfway up the street you'll find goat cheese, aged one, two, three days, or a week. Buy it according to your preference for the degree of ripeness. Older cheeses have wrinkled brown faces and flecks of gray-green mold, qualities that endear them to cheese-lovers. After you make your selection, each precious round is garnished with a sprig of savory and wrapped neatly in a piece of waxed paper.

Across the street is a fine bakery. It does a brisk business on market day, and rarely has a baguette or *ficelle* left by noon. Ask for a loaf of *pain de malt* (malt bread) to go with your goat cheese. A cold glass of *vin rosé* will complement them. You can buy it at the top of the street, in the Bar des Amis. (Part of its popularity is due to the fact that tickets are sold here for the PMU, or Pari-Mutuel, the national system for betting on the horse races.) Speak up when you ask for change at the bar—*grandmère* is hard of hearing. The shady terrace overlooks a small square normally used for parking. On market day, stands are set up here with vegetables, yard goods, flowering plants, and used books. During hunting season, the

Facing page: Four quail to grill and serve on *tapenade* croutons.

10

Grilled Quail with Green Onions and Tapenade Croutons
CAILLES GRILLÉES SUR CROÛTES

The easy availability of fresh quail in the markets of Provence is a delight. These plump little birds can be prepared in many different ways. We cook them with cherries, or herbs and bacon, and, as in this recipe, with tapenade. *Serve them as a first or a main course.* SERVES 4.

4 quail
Bouquet garni: 1 fresh parsley sprig, 1 bay leaf, 1 fresh thyme sprig, tied into a cheesecloth bag
1½ cups dry white vermouth
2 garlic cloves, crushed
3 juniper berries, crushed
Four ¾-inch-thick slices from a wide loaf of French bread
Olive oil for brushing, plus 2 teaspoons
20 green onions, chopped, or small boiling onions, cut in quarters
Tapenade (recipe below)
2 tablespoons chopped fresh parsley

Cut each quail down the back. Press to flatten each bird. Put the quail in a plastic bag with the bouquet garni and pour in the vermouth. Add the garlic and juniper berries. Put the bag in a shallow dish and refrigerate for several hours. Dry the bread slices in a 325°F oven for 20 minutes. Brush the slices with olive oil and brown under the broiler on each side. Set aside.

Remove the quail from the marinade, pat dry with paper towels, and allow them to come to room temperature. Prepare a charcoal fire or preheat a broiler. Strain the marinade into a bowl and reserve. In a large sauté pan over medium heat, heat the 2 teaspoons of olive oil and sauté the onions or boiling onions for 10 minutes, shaking the pan to cook them evenly. Add the marinade to the pan and cook gently to reduce the liquid slightly. Grill the quail for 3 minutes on each side.

To serve, spread the croutons with *tapenade.* Put a quail on each crouton. Divide the onions and their juice over the quail. Garnish with parsley.

Tapenade
Makes about 2 cups

1 cup pitted oil-cured black olives
½ cup capers, drained
3 anchovy fillets
1 large garlic clove
5 tablespoons olive oil
1 tablespoon fresh lemon juice
Freshly ground black pepper to taste

Put the olives, capers, anchovies, and garlic clove in a blender and puree. With the motor running, add the olive oil 1 tablespoon at a time. Add the lemon juice and black pepper. In some parts of Provence, canned tuna fish (about ⅓ cup) and fresh basil leaves are added.

game seller will be here, with rows of hares and game birds swinging by their feet from his awning.

After the first of November, truffles begin to appear. The harvest of truffles has fallen off dramatically from what it was half a century ago. The Luberon, however, is still one of the largest producing areas in France—larger even than the Périgord, which is known for its dishes made with truffles. Efforts are underway to revitalize the industry by replanting oak trees and placing truffle spores on the roots, where they thrive. Carpentras is the major truffle market in Provence (see the chapter on L'Isle-sur-la-Sorgue), but we've usually found ours through local contacts. Monsieur Courroux, a former goat herder in Cadenet, once sold truffles he found in places known only to him. When he retired (he's eighty-three now), we lost our source.

Five kilometers east of Cadenet is the village of Villelaure, one of the main centers of asparagus production in Provence. The village is known for its green asparagus, which begins to appear in local markets in April. White asparagus is less common; the best comes from the *département* of Var, especially around Nice. It too is available in the markets, though most is shipped to northern France

Facing page: Weekend hunters stalk rabbits and pheasants in woods and hedgerows.

HUNTING SEASON IN PROVENCE

One attitude French people share with Americans is their insistence on individual rights. This is especially true of hunters, who have been locked in a controversy with defenders of animal rights and environmental activists over questions of what game should be hunted, for how long, and under what conditions. Game of all kinds is scarce in France, partly because it has been so heavily hunted.

Travelers need to know the dates and rules of the hunting season in Provence, as any walk through live oak and pine forests will reveal the intensity of the French passion. A litter of shotgun shells is a common sight, and the sound of gunfire early in the morning is a predictable intrusion on an otherwise tranquil scene. Wild game on the menus of local restaurants depends partly on the success of hunters, though many game animals are now raised commercially.

The hunting season for all birds and beasts begins the second Sunday in September and continues until the second Sunday in January. However, the *grive*, or thrush, can be shot until the end of February. The Frenchman's powerful desire to hunt this hapless bird is hard for foreigners to understand. It helps to know that in France one says, *"Faute de grives, on mange des merles"* ("For lack of thrushes, we eat blackbirds"), meaning that any bird is better than none.

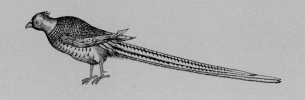

and Germany, where it is preferred to the green.

Cadenet lies against the southern flank of a large flat-topped hill covered with a pine forest and full of pleasant trails. The ruined château at the southernmost promontory of this hill offers a splendid view of Mont Sainte-Victoire, the subject of many of Paul Cézanne's paintings. The cherries that so excite painters of the Provençal countryside grow in great profusion all over the valley of the Durance. From late May until the middle of June, ladders with splayed legs gather around the trees like praying mantises. Baskets heaped with glowing *bigarreaux, napoléons, hedelfingers,* and *coeurs-de-pigeons* are piled in

(continued on page 17)

CHERRIES!

Cherry trees are a source of amazement and delight in the gardens and on the hillsides of Provence. Near the end of April, the craggy trees explode with white blossoms. Armies of bees do their work early. Spring rain and the ever-warming sun continue the alchemy. By mid-June, the trees are laden with fruit. Dark cherries, black as olives, ripen first. The yellow-red varieties that are higher in acid are picked later for the canning factories. A tree in one's garden may produce a hundred pounds or more of fruit, creating a big demand to be used.

Cherries with Sabayon Brûlé
CÉRISES AU SABAYON BRÛLÉ

It's hard to improve on the taste of a ripe cherry, but the play of flavors and textures in this dish comes close. SERVES 4.

4 cups pitted fresh cherries (about 2 pounds before pitting)
¾ cup Beaumes de Venise or other sweet white wine
6 egg yolks
1 tablespoon cold water
½ cup superfine granulated sugar or sifted confectioners' sugar
¼ cup packed brown sugar

In a large saucepan, combine the cherries and Beaumes de Venise. Slowly bring to a boil over medium heat. Remove from the heat and drain the cherries in a sieve over a bowl to reserve the cooking liquid. Put the egg yolks, water, and sugar in the top of a double boiler and whisk over barely simmering water. Do not let the water boil, or the eggs will curdle. When the eggs are frothy, gradually whisk in the reserved cooking liquid, beating constantly. When the mixture thickens and makes a slowly dissolving ribbon on its surface when lifted with the whisk, remove from the heat. Set the pan in a bowl of ice water and continue to beat the mixture until it is cool.

Preheat the broiler. Divide the cherries among 4 shallow flame-proof and ovenproof ramekins and cover with the sabayon. With the back of a spoon, press the brown sugar through a sieve to evenly cover the sabayon. Put the ramekins under the broiler about 2 inches from the heat. Watch closely and remove in about 2 minutes, when the sugar has melted. Serve at once.

Facing page: Cherry pickers climb wide-legged ladders to harvest the crop at the peak of ripeness. *Top:* A friendly truck driver with a load of cherries thanks us for moving over on a narrow road. *Above:* Cherries are one of the summer glories of Provence.

(continued from page 13)

trucks and wagons for the trip to the canning factories in Apt or the rail distribution center in Châteaurenard.

If you're looking for a restaurant meal, it's not wise to trust the advertising on the main roads into and around the villages. Once in place, billboards survive all manner of financial reverses. Whether you're looking for something special or just an honest, inexpensive meal, there are some good alternatives within a few minutes' drive of Cadenet. Lourmarin, four kilometers north, is known primarily for its sixteenth-century château, but it has a number of interesting restaurants. Albert Camus made his home here after he left Algeria. He and his wife are buried in the local cemetery, and their graves have become a destination for literary pilgrims.

Among the restaurants, La Fenière is somewhat trendy, with its Art Deco rooms and tuxedo-clad maître d'hôtel. Prices are high for village dining, but the food is beautifully prepared and presented by one of the first women chefs in the country, Reine Samut. She does magical things with asparagus when it's in season, and the veal can be extraordinary. Le Moulin de Lourmarin, a small inn and restaurant converted

Left: Lourmarin, one of the most beautiful villages in Provence, seen against the Grand Luberon.

from an old olive-oil mill, is located across from the soccer field, and there's plenty of parking. Read the menu before you go in. These are not simple dishes, but if the prices don't deter you, the meal is sure to please. Restaurant Michel-Ange in La Maison Ollier, in the center of the village, changed hands in 1993. The new focus is Italian-style food and modest local wines. In hot weather the candlelit tables on the open terrace in the back are cool and intimate. The Agneau Gourmand, a few kilometers east of Lourmarin on the road to Vaugines, offers an elegant setting and classic French food.

Four or five small bistro-type restaurants with inside and outside service can be found near the center of the village and in the environs. We especially like La Louche au Beurre for a dinner of steak and *pommes frites* with a sturdy local red wine. Le Paradou, just outside Lourmarin in the direction of Bonnieux, serves a good meal on a vine-shaded terrace. Simple, inexpensive rooms are also available there.

Other Monday markets in Provence: Bédarrides, Bédoin, Bollene, Cavaillon, Fontvieille, Forcalquier, Goult, Lauris, Mazan, Nîmes, Piolenc, Saint-Didier, Saint-Saturnin-les-Avignon, Tulette

TUESDAY IN LA TOUR D'AIGUES
A Château Market

La Tour d'Aigues was the principal castle town of the eastern Luberon until the French Revolution. Farmers and artisans were drawn here to provide the goods and services that the wealth of a noble family could demand. The castle was sacked and burned by the townspeople during the French Revolution. With the birth of the Fifth Republic in 1958 came a new sense of pride in French history and culture, and the towering walls of the château were partially restored.

As it graces the town around it, the château also lends a certain romance to the Tuesday market that spreads out before it. A large open square on the south side, used for parking the rest of the week, on Tuesday hosts the stalls and trailers of a market that offers considerable diversity and competitive prices. We like to shop for vegetables here: Lanky leeks; tomatoes with the bumpy, awkward look of vine-ripened fruit; and inky eggplant are our favorites.

Facing page: The Tuesday market in La Tour d'Aigues, in the wide, shady square in front of the château. *Above:* The partially restored château of La Tour d'Aigues, seen from the vineyards below it.

No meal in Provence is complete without its vegetable course, and produce so fresh and fine calls for simple preparation. We think leeks are best at room temperature, with only a vinaigrette dressing. A steam bath pops off tomato skins, leaving tomatoes ready for seeding, chopping, and spreading over hot pasta. A few minutes on the grill suffices for thick slices of eggplant that have been salted to pull out the water, then coated with olive oil. Some fresh radishes (don't forget the butter and salt) add zest to any meal. Indeed, this may be the garden of earthly delights we've always heard of.

We've tried many of the sausages that come into the markets from the foothills of the Alps, visible on a clear day from the château, and from the Ardèche across the Rhône River to the northwest. Most are made of pork, flavored with green pepper or garlic, and sometimes rolled in herbs. There are sausages made of donkey and bull meat too, which we've tasted

Facing page: Tomato crates perched on the château wall overlooking the fertile valley of the Pays d'Aigues. *Above:* Mild, flavorful radishes await fresh butter and salt to transform them into a magical appetizer. *Right:* Leeks cooked and served at room temperature with a mild vinaigrette make a wonderful starter for a meal.

21

but view with alarm. The French typically make a sandwich of sliced sausage on a buttered baguette, or serve sausage slices with olives or gherkins as an appetizer.

Though not a large town, La Tour d'Aigues retains a sense of importance from the days when it played a significant role in the life of the region. In recognition of its noble past, over the last ten years departmental authorities have provided funds for a partial restoration of the château, rebuilding the cellars to make a cool, well-lighted vaulted display and meeting space and providing a small outdoor theater in the courtyard. The town government has organized a busy program of activities, with seminars and exhibitions throughout the year, and summer theatrical events.

On a typical Tuesday, the square in La Tour d'Aigues is full of shoppers but has plenty of elbow room, a consequence of the ample site and the logical layout. Things get more congested near the road, as cars disgorge or collect shoppers. There's adequate parking, thanks to the château's program. Across the street from the market is the Café du Château. On market days, it epitomizes the type, with its long

Top: Financial assistance from the government has made it possible to rebuild part of this château, which was burned during the French Revolution. *Left:* In the shade of an umbrella, a careful shopper picks only the best tomatoes. *Facing page:* Haricots verts and homemade sausage.

Salad of Green Beans, Sausage, and Bacon

SALADE D'HARICOTS
VERTS, SAUCISSON, ET
LARDONS

In June, the green beans in the markets are thin, long, and velvety. Make this salad for a first course, or for a picnic. You can find sausages in every market; the vendor will offer samples to help you make a selection.
SERVES 4 TO 6.

1¾ pounds fresh green beans
1 teaspoon salt
3 ounces dry sausage or salami, cut into thick slices and then into strips (about ½ cup)
4 bacon slices, cooked crisp, drained, and crumbled
3 tablespoons pine nuts, lightly toasted in a dry skillet

Vinaigrette
2 tablespoons olive oil
1 tablespoon red wine vinegar
1 tablespoon Dijon mustard
Salt and freshly ground pepper to taste

Trim the stem ends from the beans and cut them into 2-inch pieces. In a large saucepan, bring 6 cups of water to a rolling boil. Add the salt and drop in the beans. Cook over high heat for about 4 minutes, or until the beans are tender but crisp; do not overcook. Place in a colander under cold running water to stop the cooking. Shake the colander to drain. Put the green beans in a large bowl along with the sausage, bacon, and pine nuts. Whisk the vinaigrette ingredients together in a small bowl and pour over the salad ingredients. Toss gently and serve.

copper-covered bar, black and white tiled floor, smoky atmosphere heavy with the scent of French cigarettes, and subdued but insistent background music from a local rock station. It also offers a slice of French country life worth closer inspection.

When we look in, a young mother is hauling a hefty basket of groceries with one arm and a recalcitrant child with the other. Someone's little girl is trying out new roller skates with Day-Glo green plastic wheels. A disheveled waitress hustles coffee and stronger drinks, while behind the bar the mistress of the house, a sober-looking woman, keeps a cool, practiced eye on the flow of business.

At scarred tables and in booths, half a dozen older men nurse glasses of wine or *pastis* as they debate the merits of the day's urgent issues. Listen to the local accent. You'll begin to catch bits and pieces of their conversation. It may be about the continuing decay of Marseilles, last night's soccer match, or the perennial favorite, local politics. Whatever the topic, this group is the heart and soul of the café. The look of the land is on them; they all wear caps and jackets indoors, and most have eyeglasses and graying hair. Their hands and faces, dark from the sun,

Above: Some of the basic ingredients for a ratatouille, arranged to tempt the passing shopper. *Facing page:* The Château de Mille winery.

Ratatouille with Poached Quail Eggs
RATATOUILLE AUX OEUFS POCHÉS

This dish is quintessentially Provençal, using most of the vegetables associated with this sunny land. As with bouillabaisse, *everyone thinks he or she has the* véritable *recipe. Baskets of spotted quail eggs are often available in the markets of Provence. If you can't find them, use small chicken eggs instead. Make this dish a day ahead, if possible, as the flavors improve.* SERVES 8 AS A FIRST COURSE OR 6 AS A MAIN COURSE.

2 large eggplants or 3 small ones, cut into 1-inch cubes
5 to 6 zucchini, cut into 1-inch slices
Salt for sprinkling
½ cup olive oil or more as needed, plus olive oil for drizzling
4 yellow onions, coarsely chopped
2 red and 2 green sweet peppers, seeded, deribbed, and cut into thin slices
5 to 6 garlic cloves, chopped
6 tomatoes, peeled, seeded, and coarsely chopped
1 rounded tablespoon minced fresh parsley

1 teaspoon dried basil
1 teaspoon dried thyme
1 bay leaf
Freshly ground black pepper to taste
2 large yellow sweet peppers
6 to 8 quail or small chicken eggs
Six to eight ¾-inch-thick slices from a wide loaf of French bread, toasted and brushed with olive oil
Fresh basil leaves for garnish
Black olives for garnish

Put the eggplant cubes and zucchini slices in a colander. Sprinkle salt on them, turning them with your hands to distribute the salt. Let them drain for 30 minutes. Quickly rinse off the salt under running water. Blot the vegetables dry with paper or cloth towels.

In a large skillet or heavy kettle over medium heat, heat 2 tablespoons of the olive oil and cook the eggplant and zucchini, turning frequently until the cubes are lightly browned. Transfer to a large bowl. Heat another 2 tablespoons of the olive oil and cook the onions for 4 minutes. Add the red and green peppers, stirring with a wooden spatula so they cook evenly and begin to brown, adding olive oil as needed. Add the garlic and cook for 1 minute. Transfer to the large bowl with the eggplant and zucchini. Clean the pan of any dark or burned bits, and return all the vegetables to the pan. Add the tomatoes, herbs, black pepper, and any remaining olive oil. Simmer uncovered, for 30 to 40 minutes, carefully stirring from time to time. If there is excessive juice, dip it out with a cup, pour it into a saucepan, cook over high heat to reduce, and return it to the ratatouille.

Meanwhile, put the yellow peppers under a broiler and char on all sides. Put the peppers in a paper bag and close it. Let sit for 15 minutes, then peel the charred skin from the peppers and remove the seeds. Cut the peppers into strips, place the strips in a bowl, and drizzle with olive oil. Fill a sauté pan half full of water and bring it to a simmer. Crack 1 egg into a small bowl and slip it into the pan. Repeat with the remaining eggs. Cook gently for 4 minutes. Remove with a slotted spoon and set aside in a bowl of warm water.

To serve, put 1 crouton on each plate. Mound the ratatouille, hot or cold, on the crouton. Surround the vegetables with the yellow pepper strips. Put a poached quail or chicken egg in an indentation on top. Garnish with basil leaves and black olives, and *voilà!* The taste and color of Provence.

are deeply lined: You feel the soil of Provence must be there in the cracks.

No road or path in this part of Provence goes far without passing through vineyards. The wine cooperative of La Tour d'Aigues is open every day of the week including Sunday morning. They bottle a reputable and inexpensive red wine under the label Cellier de Marrenon. Like the celebrated wines of Châteauneuf-du-Pape, the red wines of the Côtes du Luberon are made from a mixture of grapes, principally Grenache, for its hardiness and ability to produce alcohol; Cinsault, for its productivity; and Syrah, for its ruby color, earthy flavor, and depth. Other varieties used include Mourvèdre, Gamay, and Counoise.

Though you may arrive in Provence with little appreciation for *vin rosé*, it's hard to imagine that you could leave with the same attitude. These crisp, fruity cherry-tinted wines, low in alcohol and most pleasing when served chilled, enhance the foods of the region with sincerity and charm. The white wines, made principally from Ugni Blanc, Clairette, and Bourboulenc grapes (with small amounts of Grenache Blanc, Marsanne, and Roussanne) are rather tentative in flavor and short-lived. We have, however, found one or two that consistently please (see "Wines of the Luberon," page 27).

(continued on page 28)

WINES OF THE LUBERON

The local wines complement and enhance the food that comes from the soil of this wonderfully complex land. *Vins ordinaires,* or table wines, are short-lived, modest in alcohol, and made from grapes grown locally and brought to the village *coopérative* for crushing and vinification. The products of small, independent producers are known as *château* wines.

Château Turcan, east of Cadenet near Ansouis, makes a white wine with a distinctive floral aroma, and a crisp rosé that we drink with summer lunches. Château de Sannes, also not far from Ansouis, makes an organic red wine that we have happily consumed after keeping it for five years in our cellar. Château La Verrerie, west of Cadenet in Puget-sur-Durance, produces a lovely white wine, mainly of Bourboulenc grapes, and a full-bodied red wine that local restaurants have been putting away for future consumption. On the way from Bonnieux to Apt, a wine stop at Château La Canorgue is recommended, and many who live nearby swear by the wines of Château des Milles.

Aix-en-Provence wines are designated Côteaux d'Aix-en-Provence under the French labeling law, known as *Appellation d'Origine Controlée,* or AOC. The tiny Palette area, close to the southern outskirts of Aix, produces an excellent white wine. In Rians, northeast of Aix, Château Vignelaure has gained recognition for its Bordeaux-style reds. The white wine of Cassis and the rosé of Bandol, on the coast, are esteemed by wine-lovers. The chalky soil of the Alpilles give the grapes a distinctive flavor, and in 1995, the region was granted its own AOC designation, Vins des Beaux-de-Provence. A sweet wine made from the Muscat grape in the village of Beaumes-de-Venise, near the slopes of Mont Ventoux, has enjoyed *appellation controlée* status for some time.

Red Wine Kir
LE KIR PROVENÇAL

This is a variation on the classic Kir, made with white wine and crème de Cassis. The ingredients in this instance are crème de mûre (black-berry liqueur) and a light red wine from the Côte de Ventoux or the Côteau d'Aix-en-Provence.

Chill the wine and the *crème de mûre.* Pour a small amount of *crème de mûre* (1 teaspoon or less) into a standard red-wine glass, add chilled wine, and serve. This drink is sometimes called *Le Cardinal* or *Le Communiste,* for obvious reasons.

Facing page: Wine bars like Le Caveau de la Tour de L'Isle are growing in popularity. It's a nice place to visit after a market. *Above:* A vineyard near Lourmarin, and a sign for *vin ordinaire.*

(continued from page 25)

When you leave La Tour d'Aigues this Tuesday morning, go west past the little lake called Étang de la Bonde to the village of Cucuron, recognizable by its two-humped hill, one topped by a church, the other by the remains of a dungeon and a château. Local legend says that the charming name of this village is either the twice-repeated ancient word *kuk,* meaning small hill, or derived from its resemblance to the two humps of a monk's hood, known as a *cuculle.*

This market is distinguished by its remarkably pleasant site, especially the wonderful *étang,* a pond as big as an Olympic swimming pool that makes this one of the coolest places in the Luberon in summer. About four feet deep, lying on a north-south axis, the spring-fed body of jade-colored water has been an oasis for villagers and visitors since the thirteenth century. Its splendor is enhanced by a majestic double row of plane trees, trimmed so that six or eight branches soar heavenward from a woody ball eight or ten feet above the ground.

When the branches of these two dozen trees are in full leaf, the high,

Below: The land east of La Tour d'Aigues. *Facing page:* These Cavaillon melons were offered to us when this photograph was taken.

Cavaillon Melons with Beaumes de Venise

MELONS DE CAVAILLON
AVEC BEAUMES DE VENISE

Beaumes de Venise is a sweet white wine made in the village of the same name, from the Muscat grape. A California dessert wine made from the Muscat grape can replace it, if Beaumes de Venise is not available. This simple dessert is delicious on a hot summer evening. SERVES 4 TO 6.

Cut 2 or 3 chilled melons in half and remove the seeds. Pour in a generous amount of chilled Beaumes de Venise. Garnish each with a sprig of mint and serve.

fluttering canopy holds a mass of cool air that protects the *étang* and its visitors from the blast of summer sun. A café by the water is called, as one would expect, Bar de l'Étang. Some plastic tables and chairs have been set out for shoppers who want to stop for a rest, a chat, a croissant, and a cup of coffee.

Cucuron is designed for strolling. Go in by the east gate in the old wall; in spring, the crumbling rampart is crowned with irises and poppies, in summer and fall by field grasses. Wander up to the main square, where a hexagonal fountain puts forth spring water, then west along the Rue de l'Église, under the arch of the clock tower, to the old walled citadel, where villagers have planted small vegetable and flower gardens among the ruins.

Cucuron's wide streets are sunny and inviting. The village has few of the narrow, dark alleys between close-set buildings that are common elsewhere in Provence. Constructed of soft golden limestone that grows gray and flaky with age, these buildings have the architectural homogeneity that is so visible and so pleasing throughout the region. The village also has one of the best small tourist offices in the Luberon, with maps, brochures, and helpful staff.

Left: The splendid basin of Cucuron reflects grand old plane trees and the market in their cool shade.

Of special interest is the olive-oil museum maintained by Monsieur Laurent, the proprietor of Le Vieux Moulin, a gift shop on the Rue de l'Église east of the main square. A cavern behind the shop, hollowed from the soft limestone of the hillside, contains a centuries-old mill whose millstone, mounted at the end of an ox-driven axle, went around in a shallow trench where chopped and pitted olives were massed for crushing. If you can take a few more minutes to talk with Monsieur Laurent, you'll have the pleasure of meeting someone who is well informed about the art displayed and personally connected with some of the artists of the region.

Other Tuesday markets in Provence: Aix-en-Provence (Place des Prêcheurs), Beaumes-de-Venise, Caderousse, Caromb, Cucuron, Fontaine-de-Vaucluse, Gordes, Grignan, Lapalud, Marguerittes, Mondragon, Mormoiron, Saint-Saturnin-d'Apt, Tarascon, Vaison-la-Romaine

WEDNESDAY IN SAINT-RÉMY
A Painter's Place

Though not simply a tourist center, Saint-Rémy-de-Provence has nevertheless made a considerable investment in the amenities that attract and hold visitors. Thus, a stop at the Wednesday-morning market can turn into a pleasant day—or two, or even three—in one of the loveliest and most bewitching parts of Provence. It was perhaps the wild beauty of this country-side—especially the rocky moonscape of the little nest of mountains, the Alpilles—that attracted Vincent van Gogh, the most famous of many artists who passed this way. While he painted the people, the gardens, and the landscapes around Saint-Rémy, van Gogh did not, as far as we know, paint the market.

Yet when you see it, you can't help thinking how it would have appealed to him, with its lively movement, its bursting color, and its setting in the perfect little Place Jules Pellissier, in front of the Hôtel de Ville, the police station, and the Cour de Justice. This is our favorite place

Facing page: A few of the many varieties of olives available in the markets. To find your favorites, try a handful of several different kinds. *Above:* Storefronts in Saint-Rémy.

33

Left: Place Pellissier. *Top:* Cashews, pistachios, and peanuts, to serve as an appetizer with a glass of rosé. *Middle:* Ground spices from north Africa and the eastern Mediterranean. *Bottom:* Whole and ground peppers to brighten stews and soups. *Facing page:* The word *pays* on this sign assures the shopper that these pears were grown nearby.

to shop for olives and nuts, and the only place we know to buy cherries in vinegar. A butcher who parks his wagon on the east side of the square sells wonderful smoked ham and *charcuterie artisanale,* or handmade country pâté, ham, and sausage.

The other three sides of this square are filled with small brisk shops. The food market, in Saint-Rémy as elsewhere, wanders into the side streets in the summer months when visitation is high, and retreats to the square proper in winter. The Avenue de la Résistance is the link between the main food market and its extension into the Place de la

République. In this street, we often find painters, whose miniature watercolors of local scenery, smaller than a postcard, can become pleasing mementos of the countryside, the villages, and the market towns.

Because the town is beautiful and elegant, the Wednesday-morning market is teeming with tourists in the summer. This is fine for the hotel keepers and restaurateurs, and the truth is that the tourists add to the color and movement that make this market so appealing. Around the corner from the Avenue de la Résistance with its tables of chard or Bosc and Anjou pears, the fish sellers have

Poached Pears with Peppercorns and Wine Sorbet

POIRES POCHÉES AVEC
POIVRE NOIR ET SORBET

These cool, elegant rosy pears have the spicy bite of peppercorns.
SERVES 4.

4 Anjou or Bosc pears with stems
4 cups dry red wine
1 cup granulated sugar
One 2-inch piece vanilla bean, halved lengthwise
One 2-inch piece cinnamon stick
1 tablespoon black peppercorns, plus more for garnish if desired
4 fresh mint sprigs

Peel and core the pears, leaving the stems intact. Put the wine, sugar, vanilla bean, cinnamon stick, and 1 tablespoon peppercorns in a 4-quart pan deep enough to partially cover the pears. Bring to a boil and add the pears. Reduce the heat to low. Simmer the fruit, uncovered, spooning the wine over the pears and turning them frequently, for about 20 minutes, or until tender.

Drain the pears and peppercorns over a bowl, reserving the poaching liquid. Refrigerate the liquid until it is chilled. Cover the pears and keep at room temperature. Freeze the chilled liquid in an ice cream maker.

To serve, place a pear on each dessert plate. Press 3 or 4 peppercorns into each pear, if desired. Place a scoop of sorbet beside the pear and garnish with mint.

Mussel and Chard Soup Provençal
SOUPE AUX MOULES ET AUX BLETTES PROVENÇALE

The fish sellers spread their awnings in the shadiest part of the market to keep the morning catch as fresh as possible. Shiny black mounds of mussels wait to be scooped into a bag with a little ice, then rushed home to be steamed, stuffed, or put in a soup such as this one. SERVES 4.

1 tablespoon unsalted butter at room temperature
2 tablespoons all-purpose flour
¼ cup minced fresh flat-leaf parsley
2 tablespoons finely chopped garlic
2 cups dry white wine
Two 8-ounce bottles clam juice
1 bunch Swiss chard, washed and cut into ribbons (4 cups)
2 pounds fresh mussels, scrubbed and debearded (discard any open or damaged mussels)

1 cup finely chopped sweet red or white onions
3 tomatoes, peeled, seeded, and coarsely chopped (2 cups)
¼ teaspoon fennel seeds (optional)
Salt and freshly ground pepper to taste
Olive oil for garnish

In a small bowl, mix the butter and flour, kneading them together until smooth to make a *beurre manié;* set aside. Mix the parsley and garlic together to make a *persillade.* In a large kettle with a lid, heat the wine and clam juice. Add half the Swiss chard, then half the mussels, half the onions, and half the tomatoes. Repeat with the remaining chard, mussels, onions, and tomatoes. Add the fennel seeds if desired.

Cover and turn the heat to high. As the liquids begin to boil, shake the pan vigorously or turn the ingredients with a wooden spoon. Cook for 5 to 6 minutes. With tongs, take out the opened mussels. Discard any mussels that have not opened. Remove the mussel meat from the shells and return it to the soup. Discard the shells.

Add the *beurre manié* to the liquid in the kettle, and stir until it is incorporated. Add the *persillade* and bring soup to a simmer. Cook 1 minute, add the salt and pepper, then ladle soup into warm bowls. Garnish with a swirl of olive oil.

parked their wagons beside the peeling walls of the church of Saint-Martin. A bag of fresh mussels or a fresh sole will go home with us, for a light and easy meal.

The oldest and most charming part of the market lies within the Boulevard Marceau, following the perimeter of what once was the old city wall. On market days, the northern portion becomes a clothing market. If you need a hat, gloves, boots, or any such practical and inexpensive article, this is the place to look for it. Where the boulevard circles east, clothing stands give way to toys, candies, kitchen implements, and hardware.

An antiques and flea market occupies the Place de la République, across the Boulevard Marceau from the domed church of Saint-Martin. It's less extensive than those of L'Isle-sur-la-Sorgue or Aix-en-Provence, but it draws sellers from the slice of Provence west of the Rhône, towns such as Arles, Nîmes, Uzès, and Tarascon. A sharp-eyed shopper can find a decanter, a piece of flatware, a dining chair, a square of lace, or an interesting painting.

But what makes this market important to the traveler is that you can find something to take home with

Facing page: Fresh fish, brought up from Marseilles this morning.

HERBES DE PROVENCE

The traditional mixture of dried Provençal herbs consists of thyme, rosemary, summer savory, and marjoram or bay. Other herbs grown and dried locally are mixed with these four to make special seasonings for various purposes. For example, the addition of oregano, basil, and garlic makes *assaisonnement Provençal,* which may be used for meat dishes or vegetables. Another called *mélange salade* (or simply *fines herbes*) consists of tarragon, parsley, chives, and chervil. Herbs usually used fresh (*aromates*) include basil, marjoram, and tarragon. Lavender, sometimes considered a classic *herbe de Provence,* is occasionally used in food for its flavor as well as its aroma, but is not generally found in the seasoning mixtures sold in the markets.

Herbes de Provence is used in some of the recipes in this book, including Stuffed Leg of Alpilles Lamb, Green Garlic Soup, and Lentil Salad with Goat Cheese. It is also a wonderful addition to an omelet, a ratatouille, or a beef stew.

you. Small portable items like soap, herbs, honey, baskets, and knives are available at prices that seem reasonable even when the dollar is down against the franc. At the top of the Place de la République is a stand with a variety of olive-wood implements more extensive than anything we've seen elsewhere. If you fancy it, something as large as a kilim carpet or several yards of gorgeous printed fabric isn't too bulky to be carried off. Across the street from the flea market is the shop called Charrin, which carries a full range of Provençal pottery for the kitchen and dinner table. It's made in Aubagne, south of Aix-en-Provence, and priced reasonably.

A great attraction of Saint-Rémy is its eating places. A walk down any street in the old town within the circumscribing boulevard will take you past a number of intimate restaurants and breezy cafés. Whether you're looking for a meal indoors with silver place settings on a white tablecloth, or a slice of pizza at a painted metal table outdoors, you'll find a lot to choose from. Along the Boulevard Marceau there's a café every block or two, sometimes three together. The Café des Arts offers a good prix-fixe lunch, but we have no favorites here, and reputations change from season to season. We often like the choices on Alain Assaud's menu at Le

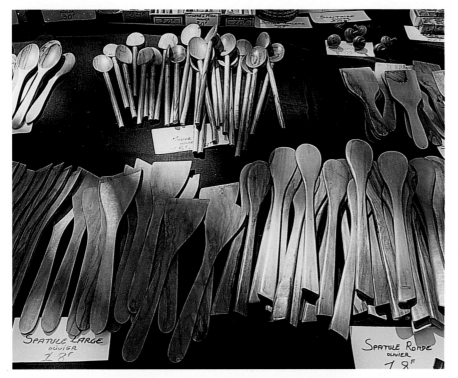

Marceau on the boulevard of that name, and the Croque Chou on the Place de l'Église has been awarded a Michelin star for good reason. The Restaurant Vallon de Valruges, out of town on the road to Salon, is an elegant place for a splendid, if expensive, meal on a shady terrace.

Our favorite place for lunch when we go to the market in Saint-Rémy, however, isn't in the town at all, but a fifteen-minute drive south over the Alpilles to the village of Paradou and the Bistrot du Paradou. Since this wonderful place has already been discovered by travel writers, we won't worry about spoiling it, and the host, Jean-Louis, is careful to protect his business and reputation. He will never let more people in the door than he can comfortably seat at the gray marble tables with cast-iron legs.

If we had to choose a last meal anywhere on earth, it would be here, preferably on a cold, blowy March day when the sun is playing hide-and-seek with the clouds. The open grill blazes at one end of the room, every table is taken, and the room resounds with quick French, rough German, and a few echoes of English. We empty our bottle of red wine before the cheese is served, but barely raise a finger before Jean-Louis pulls a cork, puts another bottle on the table, and charges us only

Both pages: Herbes de Provence, olive-wood implements, and a variety of soaps.

for what we drink. At three o'clock we pay our bill, push back our chairs, shake the *patron*'s hand, and go into the waning afternoon, surprised by how late it is but thoroughly satisfied.

If you go to Paradou, you might stop in the adjacent village of Maussane, at the olive-oil cooperative on the Rue Charlon-Rieu (look for signs for the Coopérative Oléicole). We think their oil is superior for cooking and salads. Let it be known, however, that the nearby villages of Aurielle, Fontvieille, Moriès, and Raphèle share the region's claim to extra virgin, cold-pressed olive oil of outstanding quality. We like the unfiltered oil made in Moriès, which has a stronger flavor of olives than the filtered oil of Maussane.

One of the charms of every market is the implied invitation to wander without a set itinerary, and Saint-Rémy offers abundant opportunities to do that. Yet with limited time—the constraint we feel most urgently when traveling—it's desirable to have one or two objectives in mind.

You might direct your footsteps about a block north. Just behind the Place Pellissier you'll find the small, shady Place Favier, with a cool fountain and, if you need a bite of something to keep you going until a late

(continued on page 44)

Left: After the market, the Place Pellissier regains its normal calm.

VINCENT VAN GOGH

Though he died in Auvers-sur-Oise, Vincent van Gogh spent most of his last year of life in a sanitarium just outside Saint-Rémy. According to a local guide, "From the window of his cell or in the countryside which he visited in the company of his guardians, he made 150 paintings and drawings, including several hallucinatory self-portraits, and a number of wheat-fields in the sun. In the main entry hall of the hospital of Saint-Paul-de-Mausole, he painted the famous 'Irises' the day after his arrival."

A museum in an eighteenth-century private home, L'Hôtel Estrine at 8, rue Estrine, a few steps east of the Place Pellissier, has assembled thematic and documentary exhibitions on van Gogh's life and work to fill out the picture of the artist's last painful months. We are always struck, when we return to Saint-Rémy, by the convoluted shapes of the Alpilles, which may seem to the untraveled admirer of van Gogh's work as too weird to exist in reality. Yet driving south out of the town, these extraordinary shapes rear up abruptly, revealing that even during his period of madness, van Gogh was acutely aware of the natural world.

ALL ABOUT OLIVES

Everyone knows that most olives are plump, and either black or green, yet olives from Nice are small and brown. The beginning of olive wisdom is that you don't know as much as you think. An olive is distinguished, first, by its place of origin. Within Provence, the most prized olives are grown in the uplands of Les Alpilles near the ancient village of Les Baux, and on the western slopes of Mont Ventoux, where they take the name of the town of Nyons. Olives are sold whole or broken, the latter normally at a lower price. They are either salt-brine cured or dry-salt cured. Varieties are distinguished by their place of origin, and by the manner of dressing them with fruit, vegetables, herbs, and spices. They are coated lightly in olive oil, piled in vats of one to five gallons or more, and sold by weight, measured in grams. A typical olive merchant will offer fifteen to twenty different kinds.

Above right: Gray-green olive trees, pale brush strokes against the dark cypresses. *Right:* Fresh green and black *tapenade,* to take home or on a picnic. *Facing page, top:* Nyons, Pimentée, and Provençale olives in the market. *Facing page, bottom:* An ancient olive-mill stone is now a museum piece.

Here is a list of the main types of olives sold in the markets of Provence, beginning with those made locally.

Amère: Black, bitter

Apéritif: Green or black, with hot peppers

Cassée: Broken

Douce: Green or black; plain

Douce à l'ail: Green or black, with garlic

Escabèche: Green, with lemon

Façon Nice: Brown; small

Farcie: Green, stuffed with anchovies, pimiento, or other peppers

Fenouil: Green, with fennel

Harissa: Green or black, with pimiento

Niçoise: Brown or almost black; small

Nyons: Black, tinged with green

Picholine: Green; pickled

Pimentée: Green or black, with pimiento and bay leaf

Provençale: Black, with thyme, rosemary, marjoram, and savory

Sicilienne: Green, with carrots, lemons, peppers, and bay leaf

Tailladée: Green; cut or slashed

Imported:

Andalouses (Spain)

Calamata (Greece)

Maroc (Morocco)

Tunis (Tunisia)

Provençale Olives

Start with a 10- or 12-ounce jar of dry-salt cured black olives. Put them in a bowl with 1 tablespoon of olive oil, some thyme, marjoram, rosemary, savory, and a few fennel seeds, if desired. Stir them well, put them back in the jar, and wait a few days for the flavors to mingle. A clove of garlic, peeled and crushed, can be added, but if so, the olives must be refrigerated until used.

(continued from page 41)

lunch, a charming little *crêperie* called Lou Planet. Around the square are restored buildings whose different kinds of stone and changing styles of construction tell a story of the ages— a story implicit in the architecture of Provence. On one corner of the Rue Carnot is the Musée des Alpilles, a well-organized museum of regional history and customs.

The tourist office in Saint-Rémy (in the Place Jean-Jaurès, where there's also a police station and a pub-lic toilet) has organized a number of interesting guided walks, including the well-known sites painted by van Gogh, and a survey of the town's architec-ture in the time of the astrologer and philosopher Nostradamus (1503–66), who was born here but lived in Salon. There are many wonderful rambles (*randonnées*) of long or short duration in the surrounding countryside and on the rocky slopes of the Alpilles. The ruins of the Roman town of Glanum draw crowds of sightseers. To round out the array of diversions, cycling, horseback riding, fishing, and hang-gliding are also available.

Just south of Saint-Rémy, up in the Alpilles, is the ancient town of Les Baux. In summer, buses line up in the parking lot here, bringing

Facing page: The rocky heights of Les Baux, desolate and heart-stopping.

Stuffed Leg of Alpilles Lamb
GIGOT D'AGNEAU FARCI À LA PROVENÇALE

Lambs graze on the wild thyme, marjoram, and savory in the meadows of the Alpilles, giving the meat a prized flavor. SERVES 6.

1 leg of lamb, 5 to 6 pounds, boned, butterflied, and trimmed of fat

Stuffing
1½ cups dried white bread crumbs
½ cup milk
1 egg, beaten with 1 tablespoon cold water
4 cups fresh spinach leaves, washed and coarsely chopped
4 lean bacon slices, cut into 1-inch pieces
5 green onions, chopped, including some green tops

1 teaspoon *herbes de Provence*
Salt and pepper to taste

1 tin (12 fillets) anchovies
3 large garlic cloves, minced
3 tablespoons minced fresh parsley
2 tablespoons olive oil
1 tablespoon unsalted butter
1 tablespoon peanut oil
2 carrots, coarsely chopped
1 onion, chopped
½ cup dry white wine or vermouth
1 cup chicken stock
1 tablespoon cornstarch
2 tablespoons chicken stock or dry white wine

Spread the lamb leg open and press to flatten it. To make the stuffing: Put the bread crumbs in a medium bowl and pour in the milk and beaten egg. Toss with a fork and set aside. In a medium saucepan, cover and cook the spinach with the water clinging to its leaves, just until it wilts. Drain in a sieve and let cool. Squeeze out the remaining water and add the spinach to the bread crumb mixture. Set aside.

In a medium sauté pan or skillet, cook the bacon until it begins to brown, then drain on paper towels. Pour off almost all the fat from the pan, add the green onions, and cook for 1 minute. Add the bacon and green onions to the stuffing mixture. Season with the herbs, salt, and pepper and set aside.

In a mortar, pound the anchovy fillets to a paste. Add the garlic and parsley. Blend in the olive oil. Spread the anchovy, garlic, and parsley mix-ture on the inside surface of the flattened lamb. Using turkey trussing pins, skewer the lamb together to form a pocket. Gently press the stuffing inside and skewer the lamb closed, forming a rounded roast.

Preheat the oven to 350°F. In a large, heavy skillet over medium heat, melt the butter with the peanut oil and brown the lamb on all sides. Transfer the meat to a roasting pan. Add the carrots, onion, wine or ver-mouth, and chicken stock to the same pan. Cook over high heat for 2 to 3 minutes, stirring to scrape up any browned bits from the bottom of the pan, then pour the mixture around the lamb.

Roast the lamb, uncovered, for about 1½ hours, or until a meat thermometer registers 130°F. Transfer the meat to a platter, cover it loosely with aluminum foil, and let it rest for about 20 minutes. Pour the contents of the roasting pan through a sieve into a saucepan, pressing down on the vegetables with the back of a large spoon. In a cup, combine the cornstarch and stock or wine. Place the saucepan over low heat and gradually whisk in the cornstarch mixture to thicken the sauce to the desired consistency. Slice the lamb and serve on warm plates. Pass the sauce separately in a warmed sauce dish.

tourists to see the grand view. We prefer, however, to drive or wander in the uplands, where sheep and lambs browse on the ubiquitous wild thyme, marjoram, and savory. Some say these herbs give the meat a peculiar delicacy of flavor, just as the local soil gives the grapes the distinctive, chalky character they impart to the wines of the Côteau des Alpilles.

If you're interested in sampling the wine and fail to spot the Domaine de Trévallon, best known for its

excellent Bordeaux-style red wine, keep an eye open for any of a dozen places that grow their vines in this unique soil. Our own favorite, easy to spot from Route N99 east of Saint-Rémy, is the Domaine des Terres Blanches. Their red *vin biologique* (from grapes grown without chemical fertilizers or pesticides) has demonstrated some aging potential—though we haven't pushed it beyond a few years—and a fruity freshness that keeps us going back every year for new supplies.

Other Wednesday markets in Provence: Aigues-Mortes, Bagnols-sur-Cèze, Buis-les-Baronnies, Châteauneuf-de-Gadagne, Entraigues, Gargas, Goult, Malaucène, Mérindol, Morières, Rognes, Roussillon, Saint-Martin-de-Castillon, Salon, Sault, Sérignan-du-Comtat, Sommières, Le Thor, Valréas, Velleron, Villes-sur-Auzon, Violès

Left: Sunflowers on the way south to the Camargue. *Above:* Our favorite place for lunch after this market.

THE FARMER'S MARKET IN SÉNAS

Driving through Sénas en route to Saint-Rémy's bustling Wednesday market, we spotted a sign reading *Marché Paysan Tous les Jours*. These farmer's markets are different from open markets, though they also take place in the open air. Many don't adhere to the tradition of one day a week, and they offer only produce brought in by local farmers from their own gardens and orchards.

We found this market set up informally in a parking lot, where men and women were unloading crates of produce from ancient Citröen *deux-chevaux* and battered mini-vans. Perhaps twenty farmers stood beside boxes of fruit and vegetables fresh from the fields. One stout woman in a flowered frock offered us zinnias and zucchini. Another answered our questions about her fuzzy green almonds by cutting one open, pulling away the layers from the kernel, and offering us the bland, pleasant-textured nut to taste. Three ruddy-faced men gathered behind their van insisted that we try their apricots. We did, and also admired their lettuce, which looked like full-blown green roses. When we told them we were from the United States, they responded warmly: "Ah, yes, the Americans were our liberators."

This farmer's market lacks the fast-paced commercial atmosphere of the open markets, where vendors take your order as they make change for the last transaction. Here, sellers chat among themselves and readily get involved in a conversation with shoppers. One, holding a bunch of *blette* (Swiss chard) she'd just bought, told us how to cook the dark green crinkled vegetable. "Like spinach," she said, "but add some olive oil and garlic."

On our last visit, we brought home some *lactaires*, large mushrooms with a reddish tinge, blotted by gray-green spots. Cooked gently in olive oil with minced garlic and served on toast, they make a wonderful dinner dish all by themselves.

THURSDAY IN AIX-EN-PROVENCE
The Paris of the South

Paris apart, it is hard to think of a more beautiful French city than Aix-en-Provence. Travelers and writers have noted some strong similarities between the two: the stylish shops, the purposeful air of the people, the elegant architecture, the urgent clamor of traffic contrasting with the intimacy of quiet back streets. And the energy—what Aix may lack in size and importance it makes up for in energy!

The city was founded by the Romans in the second century B.C. Because of its hot springs, they named it Aquae Sextiae, from which the contemporary name of the city comes. It languished in the shadow of Marseilles and Arles until the twelfth century, when the enlightened rule of Good King René brought it under the aegis of the French crown, and it subsequently became the seat of a local parliament. The modern city lies in a bowl-shaped valley north of the Côte d'Azur, beyond the rough range of hills called the Chaîne de l'Étoile.

Facing page: Place Richèlme, a calm and shady locale for one of the finest markets in Provence.
Above: The fountain at the foot of the Cours Mirabeau.

51

Though Aix is not far from Marseilles and shares some history with it, it is a place apart from that brawling, gritty port. Aix has sophistication and style, with upscale shops for clothing and electronics, liquor and tobacco, bedding and housewares. The cafés are constantly abuzz, partly because of the large number of young people who study at the University of Aix-Marseilles and the foreign language schools. You can hear as many varied foreign accents on the Cours Mirabeau as on the Champs-Élysées.

Above all, Aix is a city of physical beauty, which is the simplest way of explaining why everyone who visits Provence seems to come here, beginning with the Romans, who loved the water and the climate. When sunlight pours into its leafy squares, warming the bare arms of tourists at café tables writing postcards and puzzling over maps, Aix is enchanting, and you will surely fall under its spell. It has its problems, like any well-established city: some winter smog, the roar of auto traffic. But these are inevitable accessories of urban life, tolerated by those who are delighted with all the good things this city has to offer.

Among the best features of Aix are its public buildings—the cathedral,

Facing page: The stained-glass dome of Saint-Sauveur is built over an ancient Roman forum. *Top:* Two pillars of justice: the caryatids at the entrance of the Court of Appeals on Cours Mirabeau. *Right:* Plane trees shade Cours Mirabeau.

the city hall, the old post office, the court of appeals—and these are the frame for its markets. But it's also well worth the effort to search out small gems, like the Place d'Albertas, whose ancient fountain, pebbled court, and half-shuttered windows make you think of hidden openings into worlds of the past, or the Place des Trois Ormeaux, where the screech of coffee machines confirms the undying popularity of outdoor cafés and the recurring pleasure of reading a newspaper under the trees. Paul Cézanne was a habitué of the Café des Deux Garçons on the Cours Mirabeau. M. F. K. Fisher discovered it a century later, and enjoyed it for the same reason: the combination of pedestrian traffic and the little dramas of daily life that provide hours of pleasurable people watching.

There is a bountiful supply of goodwill as well as market produce in Aix. It seems a miracle that it all works so well, but the logistical success of the market results from excellent coordination between the vendors and the city administration. From six or six-thirty in the morning, men in blue jumpsuits with brooms and small pushcarts clear the market squares of trash and debris.

Left: The bell tower on the Place de l'Hôtel de Ville, seen from a narrow street. *Facing page:* The flower market in the Place de l'Hôtel de Ville, one of the biggest and best in the region.

The gutters are flooded, the walks are swept, and the whole area is prepared for the arrival of the vendors. Trucks and mini-vans begin to arrive around seven and wheel into their assigned places. Vendors set up tables and start laying out fresh produce. Shoppers arrive early to test the firmness of the melons, to fill their baskets with the best and ripest fruits and vegetables the market has to offer.

A good place to begin your visit is the flower market, which blooms around a Roman obelisk in the Place de l'Hôtel de Ville on Tuesday, Thursday, and Saturday mornings. We usually walk in from the north side because we find it easier to park in one of the garages along the north-

ern arc of the *périphérique*. It's cool and moist here, with the perfume of many flowers in the air. Bunches standing in pails of water are relatively cheap, such as a dozen tiny roses for eight or ten dollars. There's not much difference in price from dealer to

Facing page: Prearranged bouquets are popular with the French. *Above:* In the post office pediment above the market, the god and goddess of the harvest take time out for a cup of wine. *Right, top:* "Will this be enough, Madame, or can I give you a few more?" *Right, middle:* Instead of cut flowers, some shoppers buy blooming plants that last for weeks. *Right, bottom:* Flowers arranged to honor the French tricolor.

dealer, but regular shoppers have their favorites. A good selection of potted plants is available, and we usually take home a small begonia, a cyclamen, or an azalea that will last for several weeks. People who live here year-round like to buy ready-made bouquets, or have them made up to order.

Things get started around eight o'clock and wind down at noon. Nine to eleven is the high time. In the last few minutes you can pick through the leftovers and save a few francs. Give yourself a few extra moments for a brief tour of the inner courtyard of the city hall. It's paved in fat gray river stones, and surrounded by a facade of crumbling yellow limestone whose elegantly proportioned windows become less ornamental at each ascending level. Out in the square, the old post office stands at a right angle to the city hall, separating the Place de l'Hôtel de Ville from the Place Richèlme. A sculptured scene in the post office pediment proclaims the bounty of the land: A lolling, bearded god and his attending goddess are flanked by bending sheaves of

Above: Tables that were piled high with produce in the morning are almost empty by one o'clock. *Right:* Tasty, fresh artichokes; spring onions; speckled quail eggs; and fresh squash blossoms to stuff with cheese or meat and quickly fry. *Facing page:* Perfect tomatoes from the fields of Provence.

wheat and twisting vines. One leg of the goddess dangles negligently from the edge of the pediment as if she were about to step into the square below. And so she might, bringing her basket, for the fruit and vegetable market in the Place Richèlme lies just behind the building, under an enormous sundial.

Few pleasures freely available to the traveler are as satisfying as a ramble through the Aix morning market; shopping on Tuesday and Thursday is often less crowded than Saturday. Place Richèlme may be the busiest, cleanest, most elegantly and abundantly provisioned market in Provence. It is sheltered in summer by gnarled old plane trees that soar

nearly as high as the buildings. There are wide aisles between the stands and plenty of room around the perimeter. The busy vendors here don't always want to pass the time of day in light conversation, unlike those in small towns and villages, but if they're a bit brisk they are nevertheless pleasant and informative.

Produce flows from seemingly bottomless supplies. Pyramids of tomatoes are destroyed and rebuilt, crates of artichokes are exhausted and replenished, fresh supplies of freckled quail eggs and pale brown pullot eggs are revealed beneath the folds of a tarp. There are never fewer than half a dozen kinds of lettuce, and one specialist boasts fifteen varieties. When mâche and watercress are in season the market is a salad-lover's fantasy. Parsley is given away, a bunch tossed in with the customers' purchases as they go happily on their way.

Vegetables are the true royalty of this market. They dominate in diversity, in richness of color, in variety of form and texture, and ultimately in volume, weight, and numbers compared to all other foods. Here are eggplants as large as a wineskin or as small as a fist; long thin zucchini and short fat ones; squat bright tomatoes, and pale stalks of chard with leaves like elephant ears; celery hearts and celery tops; cooked beets in pinched plastic packages, and sometimes raw ones, red or white; hairy yellow turnips, crooknecked squashes, and pink pumpkins; red-skinned, brown-skinned, and yellow-skinned potatoes, some as small as birds' eggs, others as big as baseballs; carrots like little fingers or like great, forked bones; white-tipped radishes, clean as a tooth—the French eat them with sweet butter. The farmers have a passion for sorting and arranging all this, not only for the purpose of display, but because of the pleasure they take in handling such beautiful edible objects.

The little square next to Place Richèlme, near the fountain in the form of a bronze boar, is home to the fishmongers with their prodigious offerings of sea life: small pink shrimp and giant prawns; gleaming squid and

feebly waving crabs; amorphous monkfish and stiff, barrel-chested tuna. What is best about this fish market is the scrupulous freshness of the product. Some of the sellers are themselves fishermen, but most are middlemen who visit the docks of Marseilles when the boats come in between midnight and three in the morning. The catch is only a few hours in transit from the sea to the market and, if you hurry, not much longer from there to your table.

We like the stand called *Marées de Provence*, or Tides of Provence, where the servers work under blue awnings in blue aprons. Here as elsewhere, as soon as one purchase is weighed and wrapped for you, the question is *"Et avec ça?* ("What can I give you with that?"). If you want to know whether the fish is really fresh, smell it. Stand near the center of the long, low wagon where the catch is displayed. If the odor assaults your nose, it's a good sign the fish aren't that fresh. But if you draw into your nostrils the briny smell of the sea, overlaid with the pungent, particular aroma of mussels, shrimp, or tuna,

Facing page, top: Shellfish from the estuaries, tuna from the deep ocean, and bottom fish from the bays, all brought from Marseilles, only eighteen miles from Aix. *Facing page, bottom:* Freshly smoked shrimp from the Tides of Provence are ready to peel for lunch on the terrace. *Right:* Dried salted cod, pounded to a paste and mixed with potatoes, garlic, olive oil, and milk, makes the popular dish *brandade de morue.*

Shrimp and Zucchini Fritters with Red Pepper Puree

BEIGNETS DE GAMBAS ET COURGETTES, SAUCE POIVRON ROUGE

On Tuesdays, Thursdays, and Saturdays in Aix, the fish market sets up adjacent to the Place Richèlme. Vendors bring the catch from the early-morning market in Marseilles. On tables of crushed ice are large whole fish, rows of fillets, and an array of shellfish with bouquets of parsley and bright lemons. Shrimp are offered both cooked, in salmon-pink mounds, and raw in their gray shells. This recipe uses fresh shrimp combined in a batter with grated zucchini for a light first course.
MAKES ABOUT TEN 5-INCH FRITTERS; SERVES 4 TO 6.

Red Pepper Puree
3 large red sweet peppers
½ teaspoon dried thyme
1 tablespoon olive oil
Salt and freshly ground pepper
   to taste

Fritters
2 large or 3 small zucchini (8
   ounces total)
Salt for sprinkling, plus 1 teaspoon

About 20 small or medium raw
   shrimp (8 ounces total)
1 egg
2 tablespoons flour
2½ tablespoons milk
1 teaspoon salt
2 teaspoons minced fresh dill, or 1
   teaspoon dried dill
3 tablespoons peanut oil

To make the puree: Put the peppers under a broiler and char them on all sides. Place the peppers in a paper bag and close it. Let sit for 15 minutes, then peel off the charred skin and remove the seeds. Puree in a blender or food processor with the thyme, olive oil, and salt and pepper. Set aside.

To make the fritters: Grate the zucchini into a colander and toss it with a little salt. Set aside. Chop the shrimp into medium pieces. In a bowl, beat together the egg, flour, and milk. Squeeze the zucchini dry with your hands. Gently blend the zucchini, shrimp, 1 teaspoon salt, and dill into the batter.

In a large nonstick skillet over medium high heat, heat 1 tablespoon of the oil until it is fragrant. Drop 1 heaping tablespoon of the shrimp mixture into the skillet, pressing it to make a flat fritter. Repeat until you have enough fritters to fit in the pan comfortably. Cook for about 2 minutes, or until the cooked side is crispy, then turn and cook another 2 minutes. Drain the cooked fritters on paper towels. Repeat to cook the remaining batter, adding 1 tablespoon of oil at a time as needed. Serve on warm plates with the red pepper puree.

you may be sure the seafood here has not been long out of the water.

Fish dishes are an integral part of the Provençal menu. You'll see stacks of salted dried cod, used in the popular dish *brandade de morue,* in which codfish is mashed with potatoes, olive oil, garlic, and milk. Crabs and mussels are popular in soups. Several kinds of fish stew, especially *bouillabaisse* and *bourride,* are always found at seaside restaurants in towns like Cassis and Bandol (each of which produces a distinctive wine—see "Wines of the Luberon," page 27). Many small towns and villages in Provence look forward to the weekly visit of the fishmonger with his refrigerated truck. A sole, monkfish, or striped bass is wonderful when served with a white Châteauneuf-du-Pape or Hermitage

A few blocks south of Place Richèlme, in the Place des Prêcheurs, a second food market flourishes. In July and August, stalls overflow these two primary spaces and fill small connecting streets—on Saturday practically merging two markets into one. At the core, however, each is quite different. Place Richèlme is upscale, cool, reserved, and calm. Place des Prêcheurs is raucous and plain, a magnet for bargain hunters. The stalls are crowded together and produce is casually laid out. In both places,

Facing page: The market in the Place des Prêcheurs.

however, bargaining sharpens and prices soften as the morning moves toward its conclusion.

Almond trees grow wild, as well as being cultivated, all over western Provence. They are the first tree to bloom, around the middle of March, and are universally anticipated as a first sign of spring. In an earlier time, Aix was the center of the almond trade, so it's not surprising that it is the home of the almond candy *calissons*. To prepare this sweet, the nuts are ground to a paste, then sugar, corn syrup, and flavorings are added. Typically, the shape of the sweet mimics the shape of the almond itself, though larger. After baking, they're coated in white frosting, and sometimes dipped in chocolate. *Calissons* are sold by a number of shops, such as Béchard, 12, Cours Mirabeau, and Puyricard, 7, rue Rifle-Rafle (opposite the north side of the jail). Puyricard also makes some of the best chocolate candy in France. Their factory is in the village of the same name, five kilometers north of Aix on Route D14. A visit can be arranged, if you're interested.

Another dimension of the Aix market experience is the flea market that takes place on Tuesdays, Thursdays, and Saturdays in front of the Palais de Justice, next to the Place

Facing page: Storefront of a *calissons* shop on the Cours Mirabeau.

Carpentras Strawberries with Almond-Orange Meringue Cookies
FRAISES DE CARPENTRAS AVEC MERINGUES PARFUMÉES

Everyone is eager for the arrival of sweet strawberries from Carpentras in June. Serve them with these cookies, which are made with almonds, a special product of the region. MAKES 20 COOKIES; SERVES 4.

Cookies
4 egg whites, room temperature
Pinch of salt
½ teaspoon cream of tartar
1¼ cups granulated sugar
½ teaspoon vanilla extract
1 cup finely chopped almonds
½ cup finely chopped candied orange peel

Strawberries
5 cups (2 pounds) fresh strawberries, hulled and cut into quarters
½ cup fresh orange juice
1 teaspoon vanilla extract
2 tablespoons confectioners' sugar, sifted

To make the cookies: Preheat the oven to 275°F. Line a baking sheet with parchment paper or brown paper. Using an electric mixer, beat the egg whites until they are foamy. Add the salt and cream of tartar and beat until soft peaks form. Continue beating while adding the sugar 1 tablespoon at a time until the whites are stiff and glossy. Fold in the vanilla, chopped almonds, and orange peel.

Drop the batter by tablespoons at 3-inch intervals onto the prepared baking sheet. Place on the middle rack of the oven and bake for 35 to 40 minutes, or until lightly browned. Gently remove the cookies from the paper and place directly onto the baking rack in the oven for another 10 minutes. Let cool on a rack.

To prepare the strawberries: Put the berries in a large bowl. In a small bowl, combine the orange juice and vanilla, and pour the mixture over the berries. Spoon into shallow dishes and sprinkle with confectioners' sugar.

Serve 2 or 3 cookies with each dish of berries. Store the remaining cookies in an airtight container.

64

des Prêcheurs. This market is strong in glass, silver, old books, and prints. There are also some delightful oddities, such as antique jewelry and abandoned fonts of type, that we often cull in search of a gift for someone special. Those who fancy furniture, lace, and cooking implements will have to wait for the market at L'Isle-sur-la-Sorgue on Sunday.

In many ways this is Paul Cézanne's city, though none of his great canvases are here. His atelier, however, has been restored and may be visited at 9, avenue Paul Cézanne,

(continued on page 70)

Left: The small clock in the Place Richelme tells shoppers and vendors the market is closing. *Above:* A handsome door knocker from the flea market.

67

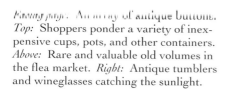
Preceding page: An array of antique buttons.
Top: Shoppers ponder a variety of inexpensive cups, pots, and other containers.
Above: Rare and valuable old volumes in the flea market. *Right:* Antique tumblers and wineglasses catching the sunlight.

(continued from page 67)
just outside the town. The brooding
beauty of Mont Sainte-Victoire,
which Cézanne painted from every
angle in every light, hovers benignly
over Aix (though you have to leave the
city to see it properly). It's a half-day's
climb to the top and back, but the
mountain has a powerful presence and
stunning views of the Alps. In
Cézanne's famous still-lifes, the tree-
ripened fruit, fat with juice, have the
same solidity and presence as the fruit
that is so carefully displayed in the
market of Aix-en-Provence.

**Other Thursday markets in
Provence:** Anduze, Ansouis,
Aubignan, Les Baux-de-Provence,
Beaucaire, Cairanne, Caumont-
sur-Durance, Mallemort-du-
Comtat, Maussane-les-Alpilles,
Mirabeau, Nyons, Oppède-le-
Vieux, Orange, Le Pontet,
Robion, Rochegude, Velleron,
Villeneuve-les-Avignon

Top left: The flea market in front of the
Palais de Justice is rich in jewelry,
silver, glass, books, and prints. *Bottom
left:* A real piece of old Marseilles or
Moustiers ware is sometimes found
among ordinary plates. *Facing page:*
Mont Sainte-Victoire.

FRIDAY IN BONNIEUX
A Village in the Clouds

It's a climb to nearly three thousand feet, but when you reach the Friday-morning market in Bonnieux, you know the trip was worthwhile. You can count the vendors on the fingers of two hands: a butcher, an organic baker, a bookseller, a cheese vendor, a clothing merchant, a florist, a goat cheese maker, an olive and oil vendor, one or two others. That's the whole market—enough for local folks, but hardly sufficient reason, you may think, to venture up what seems an interminably winding road. Yet the reward is a quiet, leisurely village, removed from the flow of time, small, unassuming, and approaching perfection in its ordinary details.

The market is in the Place Gambetta, a little square made cool by its dozen chestnut trees. In many ways, this market feels like an archetype of the weekly event that has provided fresh food to rural families for generations, a tradition as profound and settled as walking to work in the fields, doing laundry in the public washtubs, and

Facing page: These fresh loaves will disappear in a matter of hours. *Above:* The village of Bonnieux.

73

socializing in the streets. Place Gambetta is not much larger than a couple of tennis courts, but it's a fresh and welcoming place on a sunny summer morning, with its double row of vendors' stands and tiny outdoor café, the Bar du Térail.

Because it's hard to get to and the turns are tight, the trucks that serve this market are small ones. Thus the variety of meat, fish, and vegetables doesn't begin to compare with city markets, or large towns such as Cadenet and Saint-Rémy. But residents find everything they need here in the way of food, and practically on their doorstep.

If you come up from the south side, spectacular views of cliffs and crevasses are revealed, and the ultimate impression as you round the last turn is that this Provençal town must look much as it did hundreds of years ago. If you come up from the north, the village reveals itself gradually, growing larger through a series of hairpin turns. Bonnieux is a *village perché,* a perched village built on and into limestone outcroppings. But there's something special about this one, hung precariously on the flank of a mountain, on a site so narrow that many houses are only one room deep.

Facing page: The tiny Bonnieux market shaded by chestnut trees. *Right:* A narrow street, ancient stone walls, and a changing vista.

The elevation makes a fair amount of difference in the climate here. The temperature in Bonnieux is comfortable in summer, often ten degrees cooler than the valleys on either side, which rise to well over 100°F on the hottest days of July and August. The other side of the coin is not so pleasant: Bonnieux can be cold in winter, and sometimes wears a light garment of snow. The mistral comes whistling down the valley of the Rhône, straight into the exposed northwest face of the village. Anyone brave or reckless enough to stop here at that time of year will soon be seeking a warm hearth and a mug of mulled wine.

In addition to looking at the market itself, you can look up, down, and out. The terraced homes and shops of the village rise so steeply overhead you may wonder what keeps them from falling on you. Below is another street and a rather new church, and beyond are the rumpled green skirts of the valley spreading out to the north. But the sight that most consistently draws the eye on clear days is Mont Ventoux. Its white crest (stone, not snow) shines brightly on the northern horizon, changing from pale yellow in the early morning to stark white at noon to rose at sunset.

In the village of Lacoste, close by to the northwest, the ruins of the château of the Marquis de Sade notch

the skyline. Two small restaurants there serve the needs of students and teachers at the small art school run by the Cleveland (Ohio) Institute of Art. Beyond Lacoste is Lumières, and beyond that, visible on clear days, are the picture-postcard villages of Roussillon and Gordes.

Bonnieux is a feast for the architecturally attentive eye, with a richness of carved doors, embellished porticos, crenelated walls, towers, arches, and underpasses that are well made and artistically distinctive. The old church at the summit of the village is one of the finest of its kind in the Luberon. As you stroll along the Rue de la République (be alert, as it's also the main auto route through the village), you'll see a cobbled path leading beneath an arch and up a wide flight of steps, demanding to be explored. From the churchyard at the top, you can look across the valley as it dips to the Calavon River flowing beneath the Pont Julien, then rises in gentle waves to Mont Ventoux, hovering ghostlike in the distance.

When you're on the Rue de la République at the top of the village, you'll probably smell bread baking in the *pâtisserie* of Henri Tomas. He's

celebrated for his radiant personality, and for the creative way he has with bread and pastry. His specialty is *galette provençale,* made of sweet pastry, praline, and almond cream, flavored with orange zest. Fresh goat cheese from the market and Henri's round *pain de campagne* of soy flour and sunflower seeds is a match made in heaven. To accompany them, uncork a red wine from the Château La Canorgue, a few

kilometers down D149 toward the old Roman bridge. No one can claim they've lived fully until they've had these three together.

The Bread Museum, at 12, rue de la République, is worth a stop while you're in Bonnieux. Tools used in growing wheat and making bread are displayed, along with a collection of preserved breads from all over France and abroad, fancifully shaped and

(continued on page 80)

Facing page, top: The rooftops of Bonnieux, looking north to the church and the Pays d'Apt beyond. *Facing page, bottom:* Some of Bonnieux's architectural details were planned, while others are happy accidents. *Right:* Henri Tomas in front of his *pâtisserie.*

BREAD: THE GLORY OF FRANCE

In France, no meal, properly speaking, is eaten without bread, which is also an important ingredient in cooking. Breads are described primarily by their shape and by what they're made from (or the product added to them). Here's a basic guide to sorting out the most common breads found in Provence. But be prepared for a multitude of variations—sometimes shape and content are combined. For instance, a baguette may be made of *seigle,* or a *cinq-céréales* dough may be formed into a *campagne.* Sweet breads, which are eaten for dessert or on special occasions, include the *gibassier* and its cousin the *pompe à l'huile,* so called because it is made with olive oil; they have a bumpy or slashed surface. The *fougasse* is a savory bread, recognizable by its flat shape and the appearance of a puffy pretzel.

Facing page: Poppies among summer wheat. *Top:* A *fougasse* and a *campagne,* just out of the oven. *Middle:* The interior of the Bread Museum in Bonnieux. *Above:* A fresh *galette,* warm from Henri's oven.

Breads of Provence

Shapes

Baguette	Standard long loaf
Banette	Small basket shape
Bâtard	Short loaf
Bûcheronne	Flat rectangular loaf
Campagne	Round loaf
Ficelle	Very thin long loaf
Fougasse	Rectangular braided loaf
Restaurant	Extra-large long loaf
Paysanne	Long loaf with pointed ends

Ingredients

Cinq-céréales	Five grains
Complet	Whole wheat
Levain	Leavened
Malt	Malt
Millet	Millet
Noix	Nut
Oignon	Onion
Olive	Olive
Seigle	Rye
Son	Bran

(continued from page 77)
decorated according to tradition. A stone and tile oven with a chapel-style door, tended by a plaster likeness of a baker, stands ready to be fired.

Goat cheeses are ubiquitous in the markets of Provence. (See the next chapter, on Apt, for information about cheese making.) They're sold both by the regular cheese vendors who have products from every part of France, and by specialists who make and market only goat cheese. In Bonnieux, you can usually find one and sometimes two of these artisans.

One we particularly like has a small stand with glass-covered boxes at the end of the market near the Bar du Térail. He sells cheeses graded by age, size, and shape, as well as some typical products of his home in the Ardèche, where the goat cheese Picodon originated. Another of his specialties is *fromage de chèvre aux aromates,* fat cylinders of goat cheese dressed with rose hips, cracked pepper, *herbes de Provence,* and other flavorings.

The remoteness of Bonnieux and the simplicity of its market might lead you to overlook another aspect of this part of the Luberon. Hilltop villages here have an intimacy and sequestration not found elsewhere. Take some time to drive to nearby Saignon, for example. It's situated at the end of a narrow plateau called Les Claparèdes, which runs east from Bonnieux for about ten kilometers. The name Claparèdes comes from the round flat stones that abound on these heights. You can see from the road some of the igloolike houses, called *bories,* that

Above: Lavender fields in the Luberon.
Facing page: Bunches of dried lavender to scent a room or a closet.

are built of these stones. If these structures intrigue you, visit the village of *borie* houses across the valley, near Gordes.

As you roll along the crest of the Luberon, watch both sides of the road for lavender fields. Since lavender grows best above six hundred meters (two thousand feet), you need to go toward the Alps to see really large fields of it. But here at the top of the Luberon, and a few miles north near the Abbaye de Sénanque (an enchantingly beautiful place in its own right), some small fields illustrate how lavender is grown and tended for a multitude of uses, including the sachets and decorations found everywhere in Provence. Perhaps because it is so strongly identified with the region, *lavande,* or its relative *lavendin,* is

often used for foundation plantings around vacation homes and hotels. A small museum in the village of Coustellet shows how lavender is cultivated, and how its essence is distilled as the first step in manufacturing such lavender products as perfume, toilet water, and soap. Coustellet is located on Route N100 between Apt and Cavaillon, and the museum is easy to see on the northeast side of the intersection with Route D2.

Here at the top of the Luberon you're in the heart of hiking country. One of our favorite places to picnic is Fort-de-Buoux. The old fort is in ruins now, but the foundations stand dramatically on a tall spire rising from a deep cleft in the Luberon. After paying a few francs for the privilege of climbing to these ramparts, you can

spread your lunch on ancient rocks and admire the dizzying views—one is straight across to the troglodyte village of Sivergues. There is a wonderful way down from the fort by a secret escape route cut into the rock face. Another good picnic spot is the Fôret de Cèdres, on the crest of the Luberon west of the main road through Bonnieux. Among its attractions is a guided trail (*sentier botanique*), with stations where local trees and plants are identified.

Other Friday markets in Provence: Caromb, Carpentras, Châteauneuf-du-Pape, Courthézon, Eygalières, Eyguières, Eyragues, Fontvieille, Lagnes, Lourmarin, Maguerittes, Nîmes, Pertuis, Suze-la-Rousse, Taulignan, Visan

Following page: Poppies in a field near Bonnieux, a countryside filled with fine picnic sites.

PICNICKING AFTER THE MARKET

The open markets of Provence can be a one-stop shopping expedition for *le pique-nique*. You can gather a full basket of supplies, even the requisite corkscrew and knife, and amenities such as glasses, cutlery, a picnic cloth, and paper plates.

In most markets there's a rotisserie where horizontal spits laden with chicken, turkey legs, rabbit, and quail turn the meat to golden succulence. The vendor will drop your choice of bird or beast, with some juices from the roasting, into a foil-lined bag that can function as a serving dish.

To control your hunger pangs while searching for the perfect venue for your meal, buy a few slices of pizza, made to order in the wood-fired oven of the pizza wagon, or a selection of sausages made from pork, boar, or venison. The olive vendor will sell you a small amount of any kind you want. It's best to ask for a handful (*une bonne poignée*) of three or four different kinds, to satisfy your curiosity and that of your hungry companions. The bakery (*la boulangerie*) will be open until noon. Better buy two baguettes, because it's hard to resist breaking off the crusty end of one of them and starting to munch.

One of the most enjoyable places to shop is the cheese trailer. We never take for granted the number of ways the French can turn milk into cheese. Creamy, sharp, blue-veined, runny, or crumbly, there's a style for every taste. Ask for *une petite tranche*, to indulge yourselves in several different taste experiences.

Many of the vegetables in the market must be cooked, of course, but others make good picnic fare in the raw. Carrots, fennel, radishes, and tomatoes need only a rinse or a scrape with a sharp knife. The bounty of seasonal fruits—strawberries, cherries, raspberries, peaches, figs, pears—provide the choices for a light finale. And there's always an enticing *pâtisserie* at the corner of the square, just as you're leaving the market.

If you're lucky enough to have the use of a kitchen in Provence, the recipes on these pages and elsewhere in the book can be prepared, packed up, and taken with you to a meadow or wooded site. Or just improvise, and concentrate on the wonderful aromas, the presence of the earth, and the heat of the sun—the pure pleasures of Provence.

BREAD AND PICNICS

The simple satisfaction of a picnic is built mainly on the presence of bread. Whether baguette or *bâtard*, a good loaf that can easily be sliced or torn is essential. The market can provide black or green *tapenade*, sold in bulk and packed in a small container. You can buy eggplant caviar, rough *pâté de campagne* or smooth duck pâté, rich pork *rillettes*, and other spreadable products. Ham can be carved to your order, sausage and cheese sliced as you like it. Don't forget a jar of mustard. In the larger markets you can buy a *pan bagnat*, a Provençal sandwich, but it's easy to make your own. A baguette, cut lengthwise, holds tomatoes, onions, pitted olives, anchovies, eggs, tuna fish—whatever creativity may inspire—and is transportable. One tool is needed for the perfect picnic: a sharp knife. Look for a folding Opinel knife in the market.

Facing page: Picnicking with a view.
Following page: A perfect picnic site: the ruins of Fort-de-Buoux, ten kilometers east of Bonnieux.

Lentil Salad with Goat Cheese

SALADE DE LENTILLES AU FROMAGE DE CHÈVRE

This summer salad can be taken on a picnic, or eaten at home on the terrace in the sunshine. SERVES 6 TO 8.

1½ cups green lentils
6 cups chicken stock
1 garlic clove, pierced with a toothpick
1 teaspoon *herbes de Provence*
1 small bay leaf
1 tomato, peeled, seeded, and finely chopped
3 green onions, finely chopped, including some green tops
1 tablespoon minced fresh parsley
1 tablespoon capers, drained

Vinaigrette
½ cup olive oil
2 tablespoons fresh lemon juice
1 teaspoon Dijon mustard
½ teaspoon salt
Freshly ground pepper to taste

½ cup (2½ ounces) crumbled fresh goat cheese
8 to 12 slices lightly toasted French bread

Rinse and pick over the lentils to remove any stones. Put the lentils in a 4-quart saucepan and add the chicken stock, garlic, herbs, and bay leaf. Bring to a gentle simmer and cook uncovered for 20 to 30 minutes, or until tender. Do not overcook or the lentils will be mushy. Drain and let cool. Remove the garlic clove and bay leaf.

Put the lentils in a bowl and add the tomato, green onions, parsley, and capers. Whisk together the vinaigrette ingredients, add to the lentils, and toss gently. Sprinkle the crumbled goat cheese on the top. Serve with the French bread.

Peach and Raspberry Tart

TARTE AUX PÊCHES ET AUX FRAMBOISES

Boxes of red and gold peaches are usually set at the back of the market table—out of reach of fingers that can bruise their tender flesh. SERVES 6.

Crust
½ cup (1 stick) unsalted butter at
    room temperature
¼ cup confectioners' sugar, sifted
1 cup all-purpose flour
1 teaspoon grated lemon zest

Poached Peaches
1½ cups water
1 cup dry white wine

¾ cup granulated sugar
Juice of ½ lemon
1 lemon zest strip
4 to 5 fresh peaches, peeled, pitted,
    and cut into ½-inch slices

Topping
¾ cup apricot jam
1 tablespoon fresh lemon juice
1 cup fresh raspberries

To make the crust: Preheat the oven to 350°F. In a small bowl, mix all the ingredients together with a fork until well blended. Press the dough into the bottom and up the sides of a round 9-inch pie dish or tart pan. Bake in the oven for 20 to 25 minutes, or until the top is lightly browned. Transfer to a rack and let cool.

To poach the peaches: In a large saucepan, combine the water, white wine, sugar, lemon juice, and zest. Bring to a simmer and cook for several minutes. Add the peach slices and simmer for about 4 minutes. With a slotted spoon, remove the slices to a plate. Reserve the poaching liquid to poach other fruit.

To assemble the tart: In a medium saucepan over medium heat, melt the apricot jam. Push it through a sieve into a bowl, using the back of a spoon. Stir in the lemon juice. Spread ½ cup of the jam over the baked crust. Arrange the peach slices in circles over the jam, and scatter the raspberries over the top. Spoon the remaining jam over the fruit.

SATURDAY IN APT
On the Old Roman Road

Saturday is the established market day in most Western countries, so it's not surprising that the Saturday-morning market in Apt is big, booming, and crowded. The market here is spread out, as most of the town's commercial area is on level ground near the banks of the Calavon River. Apt has stood here for centuries, astride an old Roman road, the Via Domitia, perfecting its role as a meeting place between the people of the mountains and those of the plains. It was never intended for automobiles, however, and the resulting problem is described by Patrick Ollivier-Elliott in *Luberon: Carnets d'un voyageur attentif* (Edisud, 1993): "Immutable rite of Saturday morning, the market is first of all a gigantic traffic jam of cars looking for that one free parking place, while others go in

Facing page: The bustling Saturday market in Apt. *Above:* View from the Via Domitia. *Left:* Some of the earliest human-made beehives were woven from wicker.

89

circles inexorably blocking those who simply want to get through Apt on their way to other places."

On busy summer Saturdays, Apt is alive. Crowds surge through the narrow interior streets; on the periphery, drivers prowl ceaselessly, looking for parking places on the street or in the parking area on the banks of the Calavon. Men and women carrying baskets hurry to and from the market. Friends and customers stop to talk with Linda Lorentz and buy one of her renowned goat cheeses, made nearby in Saint-Martin-de-Castillon (see "Goat Cheese," page 93).

Apt is a sub-prefectural headquarters, which gives it some administrative functions in the government of the *département* of Vaucluse. A clear-headed, practical, worldly place, it sprawls outward from the knot of old buildings clustered around Sainte-Anne, the twelfth-century church. For people living in the valley north of the Luberon—the Pays d'Apt—the town has supplies not available in their small towns and villages. Apt also has the banks, cafés, hotels, and movie theaters that go with its commercial character.

The Saturday market spreads out from the Rue des Marchands, which connects the two main squares, into the many short and crooked streets of the old town. Apt is a town of tall buildings, mostly four stories, and its narrow streets stay shady and cool in

summer. On market day it's full of the rough rub of shoulders, the quick shouts, and the spatter of laughter of a busy place. Local shops stay open while the market is in progress, adding to the excitement and bustle of exchange.

The axis of the market, the Rue des Marchands, makes its sinuous way through the heart of the old town, beneath the bell tower and past the church. A few years ago, it was repaved and transformed into a pedestrian mall. Monday to Friday, the shops in the Rue des Marchands keep the street busy enough. On Saturday, at the height of the market, it's hard to make headway, and even standing still is a challenge. Rather like a small vessel, you ride the moving tide. To examine a table of goods or window display, you must edge sideways into an eddy of people or find a temporary harbor in a quiet shop.

(continued on page 95)

Facing page: The passage beneath the bell tower of the church of Sainte-Anne. *Above:* The colors and designs of Provençal fabrics are irresistible on a sunny day.

91

GOAT CHEESE: A SPECIALTY OF PROVENCE

Goat cheeses, or *chèvres*, are ubiquitous in Provence, and many variations are flavored with local herbs. *Banon*, for example, whose aroma is piquant, strong, and nutty, is sprinkled with savory, wrapped in chestnut leaves, and tied in a small brown bundle. It is then dipped in a bath of *eau-de-vie* or *marc* and fermented for five weeks in a sealed jar. *Poivre d'âne* is enriched with savory or rosemary, which gives it the fragrance of the Provençal countryside. *Cachat* is a concoction of leftover bits of cheese marinated in *eau-de-vie*.

Linda Lorentz is a goat cheese maker whose farm is situated about 1,200 feet above the town of Apt near the village of Saint-Martin-de-Castillon. On Saturday morning in a narrow, sunny street across from the church of Sainte-Anne in Apt, Linda sets up her wooden stand with a glass-fronted case of farm-made goat cheeses. Linda came to Provence more than twenty years ago. She met Claude Monge, a sculptor and ironworker, and together they acquired a run-down property from a government agency that promotes small-scale farming.

When Linda and Claude arrived, the land was planted in lavender. Conditions were marginal for that crop, so they switched to hay, acquired a herd of goats, and Linda began making cheese. Later the goats were sold to a neighbor, and Linda now buys the milk.

(continued on next page)

Facing page: Goat cheeses in various stages of ripeness. *Top left:* The Lorentz-Monge family outside the door of their farmhouse. *Top right:* These goats make milk for one of the world's most delicate cheeses. *Middle:* Goat milk cans waiting to be refilled. *Bottom:* Cheeses curing at Linda Lorentz's farm.

Meanwhile, Claude remodeled some of the old farm buildings into the modest, comfortable apartments called *gîtes* in the language of French tourism, and built a swimming pool for visitors.

As well as selling her award-winning cheese in the weekly market in Apt, Linda supplies a number of restaurants in the region. Like any kind of farming, making goat cheese is a seven-day job every week. Linda takes delivery of fresh milk from her neighbor, then adds a curdling agent and pours the milk into molds to solidify.

The small rounds of cheese are turned twice a day until they're ready to sell. The main varieties of goat cheese are distinguished by the length of time they are cured in the mold and dried after removal. One-day-old cheese is fresh. A day or two later it's semi-fresh, then creamy, then semi-dry, and finally, in a week or longer, dry. What people buy depends on what they like and how they plan to use it.

Flavor and pungency change as the cheeses age, or are altered. Some are formed into logs or pyramids and rolled in wood ash, whose chemical reaction with the surface of the cheese gives it a tangy flavor. Others, made in small molds, are called *boutons* (buttons), because that's what they look like. These dry fast and acquire a light coating of mold, which contributes its own special flavor. Dry cheese more than a few weeks old is sometimes immersed in olive oil, mixed with fresh herbs, baked quickly, and served on a bed of fresh greens (especially *frisée*).

Pasta with Garlic Cream and Tomatoes

PÂTES À LA CRÈME D'AIL
ET AUX TOMATES

Twenty cloves of garlic, cooked slowly and combined with cream, make a sweet, mellow pasta sauce. Crumbled goat cheese adds even more flavor.
SERVES 4.

20 cloves of garlic, peeled and quartered
¼ cup olive oil
1 cup heavy cream
½ cup (2½ ounces) crumbled fresh goat cheese (optional)
1 teaspoon salt
12 ounces fresh pasta, or 10 ounces dried pasta
Freshly grated Parmesan cheese to taste
4 large ripe tomatoes, peeled, seeded, and coarsely chopped
3 or 4 sun-dried tomatoes, finely chopped
1 cup loosely packed fresh basil leaves, torn into pieces

In a small, heavy saucepan, combine the garlic and olive oil. Cook over very low heat for 30 to 40 minutes, or until the garlic is soft and golden. Do not allow the garlic to brown. Add the cream, and the goat cheese if desired, to the garlic and stir to blend. Set aside and keep warm.

Bring a large pot of water to a boil, add the salt, and cook the pasta until al dente. Drain well. Divide the pasta onto 4 warm plates, sprinkle it with Parmesan cheese, and spoon on the sauce. Top with the fresh and dried tomatoes and the basil.

(continued from page 91)

The west end of the market starts at the Place de la Bouquerie. Route N100, following the old Roman road, crosses the Calavon River here and continues past the center of town. If you've been lucky in finding a parking place, you'll approach the market and instantly be swept into the thick of it. The Place Gabriel Péri opens before the town hall and the sub-prefectural headquarters. An elegant stairway in the middle of the building divides at a small fountain. Its two curves, like parentheses, give access to a balcony connecting the wings of the building. From here you have a rare overview of the market, a good place to take a photograph or to stand still until your traveling companion finds you.

Across the shaded square are fruit and vegetable stalls, meat and cheese wagons, garlic and herb stands, vendors of baskets, toys, hardware, and sweets. Place Péri is one of the busiest places in the market, with a large selection of food. Look at the huge lettuces; their leaves glisten with moisture, so fresh they might still be in the field. And the cost of such bounty seems cheap. While shopping, people constantly run into friends here, so there is a

(continued on page 98)

Facing page: Linda delivers fresh goat cheese to one of her regular customers. *Above:* Vendor with lettuces.

Frisée Salad with Chicken Livers

SALADE FRISÉE AUX FOIES DE VOLAILLE

Big green heads of frisée *look like flat, shaggy flowers in the market. Combine these greens with chicken livers and you have a French bistro favorite.* SERVES 4.

Vinaigrette
3 tablespoons olive oil
1 tablespoon red wine vinegar
½ teaspoon Dijon mustard
1 small garlic clove, crushed

1 large head *frisée* lettuce (curly endive) or escarole
Flour for dusting

4 to 5 chicken livers, trimmed and halved
4 thick slices lean bacon, cut into 1-inch pieces
1 teaspoon olive oil
5 green onions, chopped, including some green leaves
⅓ cup white, rosé, or red wine
1½ cups croutons, homemade from French-style bread

Put the vinaigrette ingredients in a small bowl, whisk, and set aside. Tear the *frisée* or escarole into coarse pieces and put them in a large salad bowl. Lightly flour the chicken livers, shaking or brushing off any excess.

In a medium sauté pan or skillet over medium heat, cook the bacon until it is brown; drain on a paper towel. Pour off all but 1 tablespoon of the bacon fat. Add the olive oil to the skillet and sauté the livers over medium heat for 3 to 4 minutes, or until browned outside but slightly pink inside. When the livers are almost done, add the green onions and sauté for 1 minute. Add the wine to the pan and turn the heat to high while stirring to scrape up the brown bits from the bottom of the pan. Pour the livers and liquid over the greens. Add the bacon and croutons. Pour on the vinaigrette, toss, and serve.

OF BLOSSOMS AND BEE WALLS

In the village of Viens high above the town of Apt, Pierre Bresc sells honey from the same shop as did his father and grandfather before him. But it's more than a shop: It's a school where we went to learn about honey, to taste it, and to understand how the ancient art of apiculture has changed, and how it has remained the same.

Most fascinating were the pictures of bee walls that Pierre showed us in some old documents. Apiculturists protected their hives from the elements—searing sun, storms, cold—as well as from marauding animals, by tucking them into niches in long walls that looked something like Roman aqueducts. In those days, hives were made of braided rushes, wicker, or pieces of thick bark, so they were poorly insulated, fragile, and easily damaged. Today, you see the same wooden boxes everywhere, from southern France to southern California.

Honey tastes of the flower from which the bees predominantly gather nectar, generally the wild species of trees or plants, not cultivated ones.

The period of bloom of the flowers, bushes, and trees that the bees visit follows a pattern from seaside to the high mountains. These periods are sequential, never simultaneous. Thus the apiculturist— theoretically, at least—can locate hives in Mediterranean meadows when the chestnut is in bloom, then move them to follow the thyme, oak, rhododendron, and lavender as the flowering moves into the foothills and then into the mountains.

Lavender and thyme are the mildest and most common flavors of honey, light in color and fragrant in the mouth. Heather, rhododendron, and chestnut are somewhat more aromatic (not to be used for flavoring tea, but wonderful with scones). Oak is the strongest: a dark, pungent honey that may be used (though sparingly) in cooked desserts such as fruit compotes.

Facing page, top: Oak, chestnut, and lavender honeys. Facing page, bottom: An ancient bee wall in Salon. Right: An etching from Diderot's 1762 encyclopedia, showing beekeepers and a variety of beehives.

Lavender Honey Ice Cream with Pistachio Brittle
CRÈME GLACÉE AU MIEL ET AUX PISTACHES

Beekeepers set up their hives near the fields when the lavender is in bloom, so the honey will acquire the slightly exotic, delicate flavor of the blossoms. SERVES 6.

1 cup whole milk
2 cups heavy cream
½ cup lavender honey or other mild-flavored honey

One 2-inch piece vanilla bean, halved lengthwise, or 1½ teaspoons vanilla extract
3 egg yolks
Pistachio Brittle (recipe below)

In a large saucepan, blend the milk, cream, and honey. Add the vanilla bean or extract. Over medium heat, stir the mixture occasionally, until it is hot. In a small bowl, whisk the egg yolks. Gradually whisk about 1½ cups of the hot cream into the egg yolks. Add the mixture to the saucepan and cook over medium heat, stirring constantly, until it thickens enough to coat a spoon. Do not overcook or the eggs will curdle. Cover with plastic wrap so a skin will not form, and let cool. Freeze in an ice cream maker according to the manufacturer's instructions. Serve sprinkled with pistachio brittle.

Pistachio Brittle

¾ cup granulated sugar
6 tablespoons water

1 cup lightly salted pistachio nuts, toasted

Butter a baking sheet or a marble slab. In a small, heavy saucepan, combine the sugar and water. Bring to a boil over medium heat and cook, watching closely, until the syrup turns a golden brown color. Add the pistachio nuts, bring to a boil again, and immediately pour the syrup onto the prepared pan or slab. Let cool completely until hardened. Put the cooled brittle in a heavy plastic bag. Using a wooden mallet, break the brittle into small pieces.

(continued from page 95)
good deal of handshaking, cheek kissing, and lively gossip.

Continuing on the Rue des Marchands, a short walk east and a jog north by the church brings you to Pinna, in front of the post office on the Rue Eugène Brunel. Pinna makes fresh pasta and pasta specialties daily, which they also supply to the adjacent restaurant Trattoria. Midway between the Rue des Marchands and the Calavon River is the large, sunny Place du Septier.

On the northwest corner is an excellent wine store, La Cave du Septier. An antiques shop on the north side of the square, called Anne Brunelle, has many shelves of old glass and pottery. If you prefer the contemporary, stroll through the aisles of Viguier, 132, rue des Marchands, near the church.

With its governmental functions and strategic location, Apt is easily the most important town in the eastern section of Vaucluse. But it has another purpose: It has long been a center for the manufacture of *confiture* (jam) and *fruit confit* (sugar-preserved fruit). These confections of whole or sliced fruit are displayed in baskets covered with yellow-tinted plastic wrapping. You can buy *fruit confit* in several shops in town, and at the Aptunion factory, two kilometers west on Route N100, where you can also tour the plant and observe the preservation process.

Above and facing page: Selecting the best artichokes and the perfect apricots.

Another small local industry is apiculture. Every open market has at least one honey seller, and Apt is no exception. Farmers cultivate bees and collect their honey in the same manner as did their forebears (see "Of Blossoms and Bee Walls," page 94). The most common type of honey is called *toutes-fleurs* because the bees gather nectar wherever they find it, and the resulting honey has the flavors of all the flowers of Provence. If, however, the hives are stacked beneath oak trees, chestnut trees, or in lavender fields, then the honey will have the flavor only of their blossoms, and will be sold as *chêne, châtaigne,* or *lavande.*

The market in Apt goes on to noon and beyond, as families lay in supplies for Saturday night dinner and the traditional family meal at noon on Sunday. Returning to their cars, men and women carry brimming baskets. They'll have food for rich fish soups, garlic-studded stews, vegetable pies, and fruit tarts, along with crackling baguettes and salty goat cheese. Like the other markets of Provence, the Apt market makes the age-old dream of plenty a reality.

And yet there is more to this market than commercial transactions—it has a social aspect as well. As André Fulconis writes: "Something more than money is being exchanged here: glances, words, handshakes, shoves. . . . For many, it's necessary to touch the immemorial market to connect again with some force, as the ancients gently touched their favorite statues when they passed them." As travelers, we don't have the privilege of sharing the sense of belonging and ownership that goes with living in Provence. But the same force, whatever its name and source of magnetism, brings us all back, Saturday after Saturday, to the open market.

Other Saturday markets in Provence: Aix-en-Provence (Place des Prêcheurs), Beaumont, Camaret, Cheval Blanc, Crillon-le-Brave, Mornas, Oppède, Pernes-les-Fontaines, Richerenches, Sainte-Cécile-les-Vignes, Saint-Martin-de-la-Brasque, Saint-Rémy, Sommières, Le Thor, Uzès, Valréas

SUNDAY IN L'ISLE-SUR-LA-SORGUE
An Island in Provence

People come early to the market in L'Isle-sur-la-Sorgue and they stay late. They come individually and in groups, French and foreign, with baskets and purses, to look, to be amazed, and to buy. The magical combination here is a setting in a fine old town with water running through it, a bustling food market that attracts the best vendors, a flea market attached to a large, well-developed antiques business, and—not least of all—a Sunday morning when people have the leisure to shop and the inclination to enjoy themselves.

The Sorgue River rises from a gaping hole in the side of Mont Ventoux at Fontaine-de-Vaucluse, the charming village beloved of the poet Petrarch. Flowing west toward the Rhône, the Sorgue splits into a skein of shallow streams whose stone-lined banks direct the waters through this town, thus its name, Island on the Sorgue. Huge moss-covered waterwheels, now serving only the interests

Facing page: The flea market in L'Isle-sur-la-Sorgue. *Above:* The banks of the River Sorgue.

of touring photographers, greet your arrival. People come long distances to this place, not only for the food and flea markets and the antiques stores that cater to the weekend trade, but also for the fabulous setting. It's a place where nationalities mingle, and sometimes vendors can be heard bantering with their customers in English, German, and Italian as well as French.

Unless you arrive early, you'll have to park out on one of the spokes leading from the hub of the town. If you come in from the south or east, you'll see the flea market first, on a wide sidewalk between the road and the water. It's worth a detour to wander under grand old plane trees, scanning tables of bric-a-brac, racks of antique clothing, and stands of books, prints, and silver. Furniture polished to a deep gloss is arranged to draw your eyes and your francs. Though these objects lack certificates of age or authenticity, you can hardly fail to be charmed by faded volumes from the last century, handmade lace collars, cut-glass decanters, silver candlesticks, Victorian lamps, and school desks that remind you of the famous short story *"La Dernière Classe."* It will be surprising if you don't find some treasure here, bargain for it, and take away your own memory of Provence.

Left: A moss-covered waterwheel in the Sorgue River.

The open-air flea market is supplemented by a number of dealers permanently installed in shops along the water and in buildings across the road. Whether you're shopping to furnish a house, comparing prices with Paris, or just having fun looking at old armoires, dining chairs, bread-rising boxes, and farm tables cut down to serve as coffee tables, you'll find more here to look at than you can see in a month of Sundays anywhere else.

Cross one of the footbridges over the pale green waters of the Sorgue, and you're soon in the main market. Kitchen ceramics can be found on the long, curving street that follows the right bank of the river. From one of the largest selections in this part of Provence, you can choose bowls and plates in traditional earthenware colors: sea green, mustard yellow, and brick red. They are thick and a bit awkward, but food looks good on them. Consider the white ware, too. It's ideal for serving dishes and place settings, and is made in a range of sizes and shapes. Sometimes you can find a ceramic mortar that's more portable than the traditional marble

(continued on page 108)

Top left: A furniture dealer and his goods. *Far left:* A knowledgeable vendor with her antique dishware. *Left:* The French use little folding chairs for their picnics. *Facing page:* The church of Nôtre-Dame-des-Anges in the Place de la Liberté is full of ornate decorations.

PROVENÇAL FABRICS

The prototypes for Provençal fabrics reached Europe in the seventeenth century from India, in the holds of Dutch and Portuguese trading ships. They were copied first by artisans in Turkey and Italy, and shipped into Marseilles. Because they gained almost immediate popularity, craftspeople there also began to copy them, and the first shop for their production was set up in 1648. A few years later a shop was established in Avignon, and from there the industry migrated to Tarascon. In 1938, a modern manufacturing plant was constructed there by Charles Deméry, who founded the firm of Souléïado. A museum in Tarascon, honoring Deméry, has a large collection of the original wood blocks that inspired the contemporary fabrics.

In most of the markets, simple but delightful fabrics in a dizzying variety of colors and patterns can be bought for a few dollars a yard. These same patterns and colors can be seen in restaurants, and glimpsed through doors and windows wherever you walk the streets of Provençal towns and villages. When they become a bit faded by use, they are irresistible.

Expensive copies of the seventeenth-century wood block fabrics are manufactured and distributed by the firm of Souléïado. Another large company, Les Olivades, has developed its own elegant designs based on the originals. Both firms have retail outlets in Aix-en-Provence, as well as some of the smaller towns in the region. Michel Biehn in L'Isle-sur-la-Sorgue has a marvelous collection of very old Provençal fabrics, and he has developed some attractive new patterns as well.

TRADITIONAL POTTERY

The traditional Provençal centers for the manufacture of fine earthenware (*faïence*), for which France is justly famous, were Moustiers, Marseilles, and some smaller towns such as Allemagne and La Tour d'Aigues. Their products were highly prized, and from the seventeenth century were found only in the homes of the nobility. These old factories have long since been put out of business by foreign competition, and current output is limited to reproductions for the tourist trade. Fine old Moustiers and Marseilles ware can still be found in antiques shops and sometimes in flea markets, but it's expensive and rarely in mint condition.

Places where craft pottery has been made for centuries remain active. Good clay is available in Uzès to the west of the Rhône, and in Vallauris near the Côte d'Azur. These are important sources of pottery destined for kitchens, gardens, and storage rooms.

Distinctive ceramics of swirled colored clays known as "false marble" have been produced in Apt for many years, and may be seen and purchased in the showroom of Faïence d'Apt.

Commercial pottery continues a tradition of useful shapes, such as the oval or round *tian* (shown bottom left), and colors, most commonly green or yellow. It is sold in most of the larger open markets. You'll also find garden pots whose upper halves are glazed green or yellow. They are made, among other places, in Aubagne, south of Aix-en-Provence. Be careful not to confuse *poterie*, which means craft ceramics, with *poterie provençale*, which means clay pots for the garden.

Vegetable Soup with Pistou
SOUPE AU PISTOU

The essential Provençal vegetable soup is made magical with the addition of fragrant pistou. *This recipe is adapted from* Provence the Beautiful Cookbook *(Collins), with Richard Olney's permission.* SERVES 6 TO 8.

3 quarts chicken stock

1½ pounds yellow-fleshed winter squash, peeled and cut into 1-inch cubes (about 2 cups)

2 cups shelled fresh white shell or cranberry beans, or cooked garbanzo or kidney beans

Bouquet garni: parsley sprigs, bay leaf, thyme sprigs, and 1 piece dried orange peel, tied into a cheesecloth bag

2 potatoes, peeled and cut into chunks

2 yellow onions, thinly sliced

2 leeks, washed and sliced, including some tender green parts

1 cup coarsely chopped carrots

3 tomatoes, peeled, seeded, and coarsely chopped

4 ounces green beans, cut into 1-inch lengths

2 to 3 small zucchini, coarsely chopped

Large handful of broken spaghetti or macaroni

Pistou

Large pinch of coarse salt

Freshly ground black pepper to taste

4 large garlic cloves

Large handful basil leaves

¼ cup freshly grated Parmesan cheese

¾ cup olive oil

In a large kettle, heat the chicken stock and add the squash, beans, and bouquet garni. Cover and cook at a gentle boil for about 20 minutes. Add the potatoes, onions, leeks, carrots, and tomatoes. Cover and cook 30 minutes longer. Add the green beans, zucchini, and pasta. Cover and cook about 15 minutes more.

While the soup is cooking, make the *pistou.* Put the salt, pepper, garlic, and basil in a large mortar and pound with a wooden pestle until everything is reduced to a liquid paste. Add some cheese and pound the mixture to a stiff paste. Dribble in some olive oil, stirring the paste until it becomes liquid again. Continue alternately adding cheese and olive oil until you are satisfied with the consistency. Scrape the pestle clean and put the mortar and a spoon at the table.

Remove the bouquet garni from the soup. Ladle the hot soup into heated bowls. Serve with the *pistou* alongside.

(continued from page 104)

ones sold in the flea markets. It's indispensable for making a proper aïoli, *pistou,* or anchoïade.

Even though it's Sunday, local shops are open: butchers, bakers, hardware, and clothing stores, as well as the Galerie Archipel at 5, rue de la République, where you can survey the best and biggest selection of postcards in Provence, from the conventional to the unusual. It also has a large collection of prints, and some tastefully selected small gifts from the Louvre Museum Shop in Paris. Along this street, a number of stalls and decorator shops offer the glorious fabrics of the region. The designs originated in India, were copied in Marseilles, and for generations were manufactured in Beaucaire and Tarascon, cities that face each other across the Rhône. In L'Isle-sur-la-Sorgue you can find a variety of wonderful fabrics at Sous l'Olivier, 16, rue de la République. We bought a tablecloth there that still has its delicious colors after many washings.

The food market is grand, rich, and perplexing, with so much to see and choose from. There are two or more purveyors of every kind of product: meats, cheeses, olives, herbs, fruits, vegetables, flowers, pottery, rugs, jewelry—whatever you fancy. The irony of this market is that it is so big, so good, so colorful, and so

tempting that you may wait too long to buy, while the best and freshest foods are picked over by smart shoppers whose mission is narrowly defined: Buy well and leave early.

In the food market, winding between the river and the Place de la Liberté, both sides of the street are lined with stalls. You can try a slice of country bread, wine from as far away as Cahors, in the Dordogne, or from the nearby slopes of Mont Ventoux. If you can't find the pasta wagon and you have access to a kitchen, search out the shop called Les Pâtes

Fraîches. A hundred grams of egg noodles will cook in five minutes and melt in your mouth at lunch time.

If you get hungry, stop for a slice of pizza from the wagonettes with wood-fired ovens. It really does taste better this way: the anchovy salty but piquant, the tomato paste with a bite to it, the crust thin and flaky. On cold days a waffle maker parks his cart

Above: Vegetables are the glory of the open market. *Right:* The country breads in the market are typically much larger than those sold in the *boulangerie.*

Figs with Caramel Sauce

FIGUES AU CARAMEL

Almost every garden in the south of France has a fig tree, tall and twisted, sometimes growing out of stone walls. The trees' late summer fruit is gathered carefully, and sometimes eaten with cream or with a caramel sauce. SERVES 6.

1 cup granulated sugar
⅓ cup water
1 cup heavy cream
2 teaspoons brandy (optional)
6 ripe black figs (about 8 ounces), stemmed
6 tablespoons L'Explorateur or Mascarpone cheese at room temperature
½ cup slivered almonds, toasted

In a small, heavy saucepan, combine the sugar and water. Place over medium heat and swirl the pan until all the sugar is melted. Simmer the syrup, watching carefully, until it is a light golden brown. Place the pan on a marble slab or in a bowl of ice water to stop the cooking. Blend in the cream and return to the heat, stirring until the caramel is smooth. Add the brandy if you like and set aside.

Cut partway through the stem end of the figs to form a cross. In a small bowl, soften the cheese with a fork. Spread open the cut figs and put about 1 tablespoon of cheese inside each one. Pour 2 tablespoons of caramel sauce on each dessert plate. Place a fig on the sauce, and sprinkle with almonds.

here, as well as a couple who sell *churros,* twisted doughnut sticks cooked in hot oil and rolled in sugar. It's nice to have something to warm your bones when the mistral blows through the market. If you need a few minutes' respite, the Bar de l'Arquet in the Place Rose Goudart offers fresh-made fruit tarts and slices of quiche to savor with your coffee.

And usually, here or in the other weekly markets around Vaucluse, you'll find Philippe, *chanteur des rues.* His blue-painted pushcart carries a

Above: Plump, ripe figs. *Right:* Philippe, *chanteur des rues.*

freshly renovated street organ. The spiked drum and the hand crank that pulls perforated cards across the lungs of the machine delight children (and us too). But best of all are Philippe's voice and the words of his songs, old ballads of kitchen and boudoir, field and fireside, including Gilbert Bécaud's *"Les Marchés de Provence."*

After the fall hunting season opens, the poultry butcher usually has pheasant, partridge, and wild pigeon. Some may come from stocked hunting clubs, but no matter—they taste just as good. In France, you must banish from your mind childhood visions of Easter bunnies. Rabbit is an unexpectedly succulent meat, always available from poultry butchers in the markets.

L'Isle-sur-la-Sorgue is on the edge of truffle country. After the end of November, you can begin to find these holy relics in the markets of Carpentras, Richerenche, and Valréas. A good place to have lunch is La Table de la Truffe in Modène, where most of the cooking is done with truffles.

The heart of this market is the Place de la Liberté between the Café de France and the church of Nôtre-Dame-des-Anges. Here are stalls of fine cheeses, ranks of sausages, ten kinds of dried and smoked hams, honey, wine, and country bread. Some remind you of the riches of the

(continued on page 114)

Risotto with Marrow and Truffles
RISOTTO À LA MOELLE ET AUX TRUFFES

Rich, delicate marrow is sometimes used to enhance a risotto. Françoise Spati, the wife of a truffle hunter, makes this risotto to celebrate the truffle season. SERVES 4.

Four 2-inch pieces of beef marrow bone
½ cup beef bouillon
2 cups green peas, fresh or frozen
1 tablespoon unsalted butter
1 tablespoon olive oil
1½ cups Arborio rice
3 shallots, finely chopped
½ cup dry white wine or vermouth

6 cups chicken stock, kept simmering on the stove
1 black truffle, as large as you can afford, sliced thin
⅓ cup freshly grated Parmesan cheese
2 tablespoons minced fresh parsley
Salt and freshly ground black pepper to taste

Extract the marrow from the bones by pushing it through with your fingers. A small knife can be used to loosen it. Cut the marrow into ½-inch rounds. In a small saucepan over low heat, bring the beef bouillon to a simmer, add the marrow, and poach it for 3 minutes. Set aside.

Blanch the fresh peas for 2 to 3 minutes, or the frozen peas for 1 minute, in boiling water. Drain and set aside.

In a large, heavy saucepan over medium heat, melt the butter with the olive oil. Add the rice and shallots and stir over medium heat for about 3 minutes. Pour in the wine or vermouth and allow the liquid to reduce until it is almost gone. Add ½ cup of the chicken stock and stir constantly until the rice absorbs all the liquid. Repeat, adding the remaining stock ½ cup at a time until the rice develops a creamy texture. The total cooking time will be about 25 minutes, and the finished rice should be tender, but firm and moist. Add salt and pepper. Stir in the truffle slices, marrow and bouillon, and Parmesan cheese, and remove from the heat. Cover for 2 minutes to let the flavors mingle.

Divide the risotto among warmed plates and surround each serving with green peas. Garnish with parsley and serve.

111

TRUFFLE HUNTERS

Jean and Françoise Spati live near the village of Saint-Pierre-de-Vassols, a few kilometers from the slopes of Mont Ventoux. In addition to being a farmer, Jean is an enthusiastic truffle hunter, like his father and grandfather before him. When we visited the Spatis, Jean showed us a photo of a small boy finding his first truffle—himself, of course. Françoise, trained as a librarian, came to Provence on vacation from Belgium twelve years ago, met her future husband, and stayed on as a farmer's wife.

Jean told us about his adventures in search of the elusive truffle. The *picon* he uses to dig them belonged to his grandfather, and the *musette* he carries them home in looks as if it has been in service just as long. His companion, Câline, a young dachshund, seems an unlikely choice for a truffle sniffer. But when Jean buried a half-frozen truffle in the loose stones of his courtyard, Câline was on it like a shot.

The truffle market in Carpentras opens in early November, but there aren't many to be had until the end of the month because the truffles don't ripen until then. After that they are available until the end of February. Many truffle hunters use pigs, who love truffles and find them readily. Jean told us (hold your breath) that female pigs are attracted to the ripe truffles because they smell like the sperm of male pigs. Another method, for those with neither trained dogs nor pigs, is to walk under the oaks toward the rising sun. When you see a cloud of tiny insects, called "truffle flies," dancing in a sunbeam, there you'll find a truffle.

The main truffle market is in Carpentras on Friday morning, from November to March, in the bar of the Hôtel l'Univers on the Rue de la République. (The truffles themselves are kept locked in the trunks of cars parked outside.) Françoise warned us to be careful to get good weight, that is, to make sure that the truffle was clean so we wouldn't be paying for dirt. She also told us that when cooking with truffles, you must be sure to use the juice, which has the most flavor. In Provence, truffles are eaten grated or sliced in scrambled eggs, risotto, and salads, and baked under the skin of various kinds of poultry; a specialty of the region is made by mixing truffles with chick-peas.

Top: A basket of Jean Spati's black gems. *Above:* A statue of Joseph Talon, the man who taught France about truffles, in the square of his native village of Saint-Saturnin-les-Apt.

sway in the swift current. Plane trees with massive, scaly trunks, some older than the century, bend benevolently above the streets. Their bark has the green hues of olives and the pale purple of dried lavender. Sniff the wood smoke from the pizza wagon one more time. It blends with the aroma of fried eggrolls wafting from the stand of a Vietnamese family. They have combined the food of their culture with the market system of Provence, continuing a process centuries in the making and still evolving.

As the clock strikes noon, stands begin to come clattering down. The crowd thins out, and you can move without stepping on toes, tripping on small dogs, or surprising a baffled child hidden among adult legs. The basket seller, his hair in disarray, gesticulates in the face of the cheese seller. The olive vendor restores each of eighteen varieties to drums in the back of his truck. Wine, oil, soap, fabric, dishes, flowers, herbs—all are stacked or bagged or folded or stowed for the trip home. The wondrously long truck of Bazaar André, with trays carrying everything from socks to spoons and whisks to whistles, retreats like a snail into its shell and crawls away. Bonnet's shoe truck, selling something for each member of

(continued from page 111)

Indies: luscious dark figs streaked with yellow, conical heaps of aromatic ground spices, wide wooden containers of freshly crushed *tapenades*. You understand as you sip your coffee what it is that makes this town so grand: generous streets that let in light and air, yet contain a mass of people as well as goods like no others in Provence.

Because of its size and the variety of what you can buy, L'Isle-sur-la-Sorgue symbolizes all that is best in the markets of Provence, the cornucopia that finally, in this century, has become manifest for the farmers of this once-forgotten region. Of course, they come here to shop and exchange greetings, to fill their baskets, their cupboards, and their stomachs. But beyond its practical functions, this market is a place where country people and their children can celebrate their accomplishment. They have provided this bounty. This food smells and looks and tastes as it does because they have sown it and grown it and brought it here to sell.

Before you leave the town, come back to the water. It's shallow, fast-moving, clean, and cool. Water weeds

Top: Marketing also means visiting. *Facing page:* Early afternoon at the Café de France, after the market.

the family, folds up like a Chinese puzzle and glides into the bright afternoon.

Soon the street sweepers are at work. The Place de la Liberté no longer echoes to the pan pipes, drums, and rattles of Peruvian musicians. The cavernous Café de France reverts to the regulars: the billiard players, the patient readers of local newspapers, the solitary cigarette smoker blowing thick streams of smoke from his unfiltered Disque-Bleu. He sips a small cup of black coffee with one lump of sugar. It lasts and lasts; perhaps it will last until next Sunday's market.

Other Sunday markets in Provence: Aigues-Mortes, Beaucaire, Camaret, Colonzelle, Châteaurenard, Jonquières, Marguerittes, Mirabeau, Mormoiron, Sorgues

RESOURCES

Other Markets

Morning markets of one kind or another are held every day of the week in Provence. One-day-a-week open markets are listed at the end of each chapter, while other open markets, farmer's markets, and specialized markets are listed below.

OPEN MARKETS

Daily Aix-en-Provence (Place Richèlme), Arles

Monday through Thursday, and Saturday Alès

Tuesday through Sunday Avignon (Place des Carmes)

RETAIL FARMER'S MARKETS

Apt on Tuesday; Beaumont de Pertuis on Saturday; Cadenet on Saturday; Coustellet on Sunday; Monteux on Wednesday and Saturday; Pertuis on Wednesday and Saturday; Saint-Martin-de-la-Brasque on Sunday; Sarrians on Sunday; Sénas every weekday; Velleron every weekday.

SPECIALIZED MARKETS

Asparagus Vaison-la-Romaine: last Tuesday in February.

Flowers Aix-en-Provence: Place de la Mairie, Tuesday, Thursday, and Saturday; Place Prêcheurs, Sunday. Avignon: Place des Carmes, Saturday morning.

Garlic Aix-en-Provence: Saturday and Sunday in July; Martigues and Uzès: Saturday and Sunday in June.

Lime (linden) blossoms Vaison-la-Romaine: last Tuesday in June and July.

Provençal products Beaumes-de-Venise: Tuesday morning from April to October; Vaison-la-Romaine in the upper town, Sunday morning from June to September.

Truffles November to March: Friday in Carpentras; Saturday in Apt, Richerenches, and Uzès; Wednesday in Valréas.

Wines of the Côtes de Ventoux Carpentras: Saturday morning in July and August.

Seasonal Specialties of the Region

A great deal of produce in the markets of Provence comes from other parts of France or abroad. The speed of air freight makes it difficult to distinguish between an artichoke grown in Israel and one grown locally. The prevalence of greenhouses and agriculture under plastic has extended growing seasons, and there is not always agreement on what is a legitimate specialty of Provence. Still, there is scant reason to deny your senses when you smell a ripe peach or press the stem end of a melon. So buy and enjoy what appeals to you!

Spring

- artichokes (into summer)
- asparagus
- green garlic
- strawberries (into summer)

Summer

- apricots
- Cavaillon (Charentais) melons
- chard (into fall)
- cherries
- eggplants (into fall)
- fennel
- figs (into fall)
- garlic
- nectarines
- peaches
- pears (into fall)
- peppers (into fall)
- plums
- potatoes
- tomatoes (into fall)
- zucchini

Fall

- apples
- carrots
- grapes
- persimmons
- quinces

Winter

- olives and olive oil (available all year)
- truffles

Typical Foods of Provence

Aïoli More than a sauce, this garlic mayonnaise is the symbol of Provence. An amalgam of garlic, egg yolk, and olive oil, it is best made in a mortar, and is used on vegetables, fish, meats, and in soups.

Anchoïade A spread for grilled bread, made of pounded anchovies, garlic, herbs, and olive oil.

Bagna cauda An import from Italy, meaning "hot bath." Garlic, olive oil, and mashed anchovies are heated together and served as a dip for raw vegetables.

Beignet A fritter of small vegetables or shellfish dipped in batter and fried.

Bouillabaisse A stew or thick soup made from Mediterranean fish and vegetables. It is served with *rouille*.

Bourride A "white" fish stew made with seafood and white wine and flavored with aïoli.

Brandade de morue Salt cod mixed with potatoes, garlic, oil, and milk to make a smooth puree.

Daube A traditional Provençal meat stew, slowly simmered for hours and often served with macaroni.

Fougasse A flat bread shaped like a puffy pretzel. Made with olive oil, it may have bits of salt pork, sun-dried tomatoes, or cheese baked into it.

Gibassier A sweet bread with bits of candied fruit or citrus zest. The surface is slashed, giving it a characteristic appearance and shape. A similar bread, the *pompe à l'huile,* is made with olive oil.

Lardons Small squares of lean salt pork. Rolled in *persillade,* they may be inserted in meats to be roasted, for flavor. When fried, they are used in salads or soups.

Pan bagnat A loaf of bread sliced open, sprinkled with vinegar and olive oil, and filled with tomatoes, onions, anchovies, and roasted red peppers. Closed, it is eaten with gusto.

Panisse Chick-pea flour mixed with water and cooked to a thick paste. When cooled, it is fried in sticks like French fries.

Persillade Parsley and garlic minced together to make a universal Provençal flavoring. Combined with bread crumbs, it makes a fine topping for *tians* or pizzas.

Pissaladière A slow-cooked pizzalike tart of onions, black olives, and anchovies, delicious hot or cold.

Pistou A sauce of pureed fresh basil leaves, garlic, and olive oil.

Pot-au-feu A variety of meats (beef, lamb, veal) and vegetables cooked together in a broth. It is a labor-intensive but celebrated feast. A bowl of chick-peas is a necessary accompaniment.

Raïto A red wine sauce for certain fish, made with garlic, tomatoes, capers, and black olives.

Rouille A sauce of chilies, garlic, bread, and olive oil, served with *bouillabaisse.*

Sabayon A custard-like dessert made by whisking together egg yolks, fortified sweet wine, and sugar, over simmering water.

Socca A thin, flat cake made of chick-pea flour; a specialty of Nice.

Soupe au pistou A soup of vegetables, pasta, and *pistou.*

Tapenade A puree of black or green olives, capers, anchovies, garlic, and olive oil. *Tapens* is Provençal for capers.

Tian A vegetable gratin baked in an oven, named for the flat oval or round earthenware dish in which the vegetables are cooked.

Trouchia An omelet filled with chard.

Phrases for Use in the Markets

Here is a starter set of phrases that can be helpful visiting or shopping in the open markets. You'll find it most useful in conjunction with a standard dictionary or phrasebook that gives some guidance to pronunciation. A portable paperback model will be available in the *maison de la presse* (the newspaper and magazine store) in any of the larger towns and villages. The response to your overtures may be rapid, and at first unintelligible. Don't despair; farmers and tradesmen are good people, used to speaking in their own way with their own regional accent. Persevere, and they'll soon start to make sense to you. The French are rather formal people, though they may not seem so when you first meet them. They always shake hands or kiss cheeks on meeting, say hello and goodbye, and use please and thank you in their social and commercial exchanges. You can add a lot to international goodwill by returning their courtesy in kind.

Good morning!	*Bonjour!*
How are you?	*Comment ça va?*
Fine, thank you.	*Très bien, merci.*
What beautiful weather!	*Quel beau temps!*
It's really awful!	*C'est vraiment affreux!*
Can you help me?	*Pourriez-vous m'aider?*
Were they picked today?	*Ils sont d'aujourd'hui?*
Are they very fresh?	*Ils sont bien frais?*
I'd like about a quarter pound.	*À peu près cent grammes, s'il vous plaît.*
I'd like about a pound.	*À peu près cinq cent grammes, s'il vous plaît.*
I'd like about two pounds.	*À peu près un kilo, s'il vous plaît.*
A good handful, please.	*Une bonne poignée, s'il vous plaît.*
Two slices please.	*Deux tranches, s'il vous plaît.*
I'd like three of them.	*J'en voudrais trois.*
Half that much, please.	*La moitié de ça, s'il vous plaît.*
A bit more, please.	*Encore un peu, s'il vous plaît.*
A bit less, please.	*Un peu moins, s'il vous plaît.*
That's just right.	*Ça, c'est parfait.*
Do you have a bag (sack)?	*Avez-vous un sac?*
Could you wrap it up?	*Pouvez-vous l'emballer?*

That's all right as it is.	*Ça va comme ça.*
How much is that?	*C'est combien?*
And that?	*Et cela?*
That's enough, thanks.	*Ça suffit comme ça, merci.*
Where can I find chicken?	*Pour trouver du poulet?*
Where can I find cheese?	*Pour trouver du fromage?*
Where is the butcher?	*C'est par où, la boucherie?*
Do you sell wine here?	*Avez-vous du vin?*
Is there a bakery here?	*Y a-t'il une boulangerie ici?*
I'm looking for some jam.	*Je cherche de la confiture.*
Is there a cafe nearby?	*Y a-t'il un café tout près?*
I'm looking for a toilet.	*Les toilettes, s'il vous plaît?*
Is there a market here next week?	*Y a-t'il un marché ici la semaine prochaine?*
Is there a parking area nearby?	*Y a-t'il un parking tout près?*
What time does the market open?	*À quelle heure le marché ouvre-t-il?*
What time do you close?	*A quelle heure ça ferme?*
Is there a flea market here today?	*Y a-t'il un marché aux puces ici aujourd'hui?*
I'll see you again next week.	*A la semaine prochaine, monsieur.*
Thanks for all your help.	*Merci bien; c'est gentil.*

Conversion Chart

Some equivalents are rounded for convenience. Teaspoons and tablespoons are level, not heaped.

Liquids (Fluid Ounces)

1 teaspoon	5 milliliters
1 tablespoon	15 milliliters
1 ounce (2 tablespoons)	30 milliliters
2 ounces (¼ cup)	60 milliliters
3 ounces (⅓ cup)	80 milliliters
4 ounces (½ cup)	125 milliliters
5 ounces (⅔ cup)	160 milliliters
6 ounces (¾ cup)	180 milliliters
8 ounces (1 cup)	250 milliliters
16 ounces (2 cups or 1 pint)	500 milliliters
32 ounces (4 cups or 1 quart)	1 liter

Solid Conversions

1 ounce	30 grams
2 ounces	60 grams
3½ ounces	105 grams
4 ounces (¼ lb)	125 grams
8 ounces (½ lb)	250 grams
12 ounces (¾ lb)	375 grams
16 ounces (1 lb)	500 grams

To Convert

To Convert	Multiply	By
Ounces to grams	Ounces	28.35
Grams to ounces	Grams	0.035
Quarts to liters	Quarts	1.057
Liters to quarts	Liters	0.95

To convert Fahrenheit to Celsius: Subtract 32, multiply by 5, and divide by 9.

To convert Celsius to Fahrenheit: Multiply by 9, divide by 5, and add 32.

Oven Temperatures

Fahrenheit	Celsius	Gas
275	135	1
300	150	2
325	165	3
350	180	4
375	190	5
400	200	6
425	220	7
450	230	8
475	240	9
500	260	10

A Market Glossary

VEGETABLES	Les Légumes
artichoke	l'artichaut
beet	la betterave rouge
broccoli	le broccoli
brussel sprout	le chou de Bruxelles
cabbage	le chou, le chou frisé, le chou vert
cardoon	le cardon
carrot	la carotte
cauliflower	le chou-fleur
celery	le céleri-en-branche
celery root	le céleri-rave
chard	la blette
eggplant	l'aubergine
endive	l'endive
escarole	la scarole
fennel	le fenouil
green bean	le haricot vert
leek	le poireau
lettuce	la salade, la laitue, la frisée
mâche	la mâche
mushroom	le champignon
onion	l'oignon
peas	les petits pois
pepper (red/green)	le poivron (rouge/vert)
potato	la pomme de terre
radish	le radis
shallot	l'échalote
shell bean	le haricot blanc
sorrel	l'oseille
spinach	les épinards
spring onion	la cébette
squash	la courge
turnip	le navet
zucchini	la courgette

FISH AND SHELLFISH	Le Poisson et les Fruits de Mer
anchovy	l'anchois
clam	la palourde
crab	le crabe
crayfish	l'écrevisse
cuttlefish	la seiche
lobster	l'homard
monkfish	la lotte de mer
mussel	la moule
oyster	l'huître
prawn	la langoustine
red mullet	le rouget
salt cod	la morue sèche
scallop	la coquille
sea bass	le loup de mer
shrimp	la crevette
snail	l'escargot
squid	le calmar
tuna	le thon

HERBS AND SPICES — *Les Herbes et Les Épices*

basil	*le basilic*
chervil	*le cerfeuil*
chives	*la ciboulette*
cinnamon	*la cannelle*
fennel	*le fenouil*
garlic	*l'ail*
hyssop	*l'hysope*
laurel	*le laurier*
lavender	*la lavande*
licorice	*la réglisse*
linden	*le tilleul*
marjoram	*la marjolaine*
mint	*la menthe*
oregano	*l'origan*
parsley	*le persil*
pepper	*le poivre*
rosemary	*le romarin*
sage	*la sauge*
savory	*la sarriette*
tarragon	*l'estragon*
thyme	*le thym*
verbena	*la verveine*
wild thyme	*le serpolet*

FRUITS — *Les Fruits*

apple	*la pomme*
apricot	*l'abricot*
avocado	*l'avocat*
banana	*la banane*
cherry	*la cerise*
fig	*la figue*
grape	*le raisin*
grapefruit	*le pamplemousse*
lemon	*le citron*
melon	*le melon*
olive	*l'olive*
orange	*l'orange*
peach	*la pêche*
pear	*la poire*
pineapple	*l'ananas*
pomegranate	*la grenade*
raspberry	*la framboise*
strawberry	*la fraise*
tomato	*la tomate*

MEAT — *La Viande*

beef	*le boeuf*
brains	*la cervelle*
ham	*le jambon*
kidney	*le rognon*
lamb	*l'agneau*
liver	*le foie*
pork	*le porc*
sausage (dried)	*le saucisson*
sausage (cooked or fresh)	*la saucisse*
veal	*le veau*

POULTRY	La Volaille	NUTS	Les Noix
capon	le chapon	almond	l'amande
cock	le coq	cashew	la noix de Cajou
cock (under 2 lb)	le coquelet	chestnut	le marron, la châtaigne
chick	le poussin	hazelnut	la noisette
duck	le canard	peanut	la cacahuète
duck (female)	la canette, la cane	pinenut	le pignon de pin
guinea hen	la pintade	pistachio	la pistache
hen	la poule	walnut	la noix
hen (young)	le poulet		
squab	le pigeonneau		

GAME	Le Gibier
boar	le sanglier
hare	le lièvre
partridge	le perdreau
pheasant	le faisan
quail	la caille
woodcock	la bécasse
young rabbit	le lapereau

GRAINS AND LEGUMES	Les Céréales et Légumineuses
black-eyed peas	les haricots oeil de perdrix
broad beans	les fèves
bulgur	le boulgour
chick-peas	les pois chiches
corn	le maïs
couscous	le couscous
lentils	les lentilles
rice	le riz
spelt	l'épeautre
white beans	les haricots blancs

MISCELLANEOUS	Divers
bread	le pain
butter	le beurre
cheese (cow)	le fromage
cheese (sheep)	le fromage de brébis
cheese (goat)	le fromage de chèvre
egg	l'oeuf
honey	le miel
jam	la confiture
milk	le lait

Restaurants and Places of Interest

We've checked these restaurants with other guidebooks, but the emphasis is on our personal experience and judgment. Eating out can be expensive and unpredictable, so we've provided a simple rating system: M for moderate, M+ for above moderate, E for expensive, and E+ for unusually expensive. It's advisable to telephone restaurants in advance, since closing days, holidays, and vacations abound. Most restaurants are closed on Monday. An asterisk before a restaurant indicates a Michelin star or stars in the 1995 edition. The restaurant listings are followed by lists of local specialties and sites.

AIX-EN-PROVENCE

Restaurants: Le Basilic Gourmand 63, rue de Griffon (M+), 42.96.08.58; Charlotte, 32, rue des Bernardins (M+), 42.26.77.56; Chez Maxime, 12, place Ramus (M+), 42.26.28.51; *Le Clos de la Violette, 10, avenue de la Violette (E+), 42.23.30.71; Le Petit Verdot, 7, rue d'Entrecasteaux (E), 42.27.30.12; Le Verdun, 20, place de Verdun (M), 42.27.03.24.

Calissons (almond candy): Béchard, 12, cours Mirabeau; Puyricard, 7, rue Rifle-Rafle; Roy René, 7, rue Papassaudi.

Chocolates: Puyricard, at Puyricard, 10 km north on D14.

Sidewalk cafés: Café des Deux Garçons, 53, cours Mirabeau; Le Grillon, 49, cours Mirabeau.

NEAR AIX

BEAURECUEIL, 12 km east on N7, D58, and D46. **Restaurant:** *Relais Sainte-Victoire (E+), 42.66.94.98.

APT

Restaurants: Bernard Mathys, 4.5 km east on N100 at Le Chêne (E), 90.04.84.64; Auberge du Luberon, 17, quai Léon Sagy (E), 90.74.12.50.

Antiques: Anne Brunelle, place de Septier.

Ceramics: Jean Faucon's Faïence d'Apt, 12, avenue de la Libération.

Dishware: Vignier, 132, rue des Marchands.

Fresh pasta: Pinna, opposite the post office, rue Eugène Brunel.

Gîte accommodations on a goat cheese producing farm: Linda Lorentz and Claude Monge, Hautes Courennes, 84750 Saint-Martin-de-Castillon, 12 km east on N100 and D48 (telephone 90.75.22.21/fax 90.75.11.65).

Honey: Pierre Bresc, Viens, 16 km east on N100 and D209.

Preserved fruit: Aptunion, Salignan.

Wine: La Cave du Septier, place du Septier.

NEAR APT

SAIGNON, 4 km south on GR 92. **Restaurant:** Auberge du Presbytère (M+), 90.74.11.50.

VILLARS, 6 km north on N100 and D943. **Restaurant:** La Fontaine, place de la Fontaine (M), 90.75.48.55.

BONNIEUX

Restaurant: Le Fournil, 5, place Carnot (M), 90.75.83.62.

Bread museum: 12, rue de la République.

Wine: Château La Canorgue, Route du Pont-Julien.

NEAR BONNIEUX

BUOUX, 10 km east on D36 and D113.
Restaurants: Auberge de la Loube, Quartier de la Loube (M+), 90.74.19.58; Auberge des Seguins (M), 90.74.16.37.

CADENET

Restaurants: Le Mirabeau, place Mirabeau (M), 90.68.37.65; Le Moulin de Sainte-Anne, 4, rue Viala (M), 90.68.28.91; Stéfani, avenue Gambetta (M+), 90.68.07.14.

Basket museum: La Glaneuse, avenue Philippe-de-Girard.

Maison de la presse: place Tambour d'Arcole, avenue Gambetta side.

Wine: Château La Verrerie, Puget-sur-Durance, 10 km west on D973; Château Turcan, Ansouis, 10 km east on D45 and D135.

NEAR CADENET

LOURMARIN, 5 km north on D943.
Restaurants: L'Agneau Gourmand, 3 km east on D56 (E), 90.68.21.04; Le Bistrot, rue Philippe-de-Girard (M), 90.68.06.69; *La Fenière, 9, rue du Grand-Pré (E), 90.68.11.79; La Louche à Beurre, avenue Philippe-de-Girard (M), 90.68.00.33; Le Moulin de Lourmarin, rue du Temple (E), 90.68.06.69; Le

Paradou, 1.5 km north on D943 (M), 90.68.04.05; La Récréation, rue Philippe-de-Girard (M), 90.68.23.73.

L'ISLE-SUR-LA-SORGUE

Restaurants: Le Jardin du Quai, 2, avenue Julien-Guigue (M+), 90.38. 56.17; Mas de Cure Bourse, 2 km east on D25, (E), 90.38.16.58; *Nicolet, 15 km south on D31 (E), 90.78.01.56; Le Pétrarche, 1, route d'Apt (M), 90.38.10.52; La Prévôté, 4, rue Jean-Jacques Rousseau (M+), 90.38.57.29.

Anduze garden pots: Easter and Assumption Day (August) weekend flea markets.

Contemporary fabrics: Sous l'Olivier, 16, rue de la République.

Delicatessen: Les Délices du Luberon, avenue 8-Mai-1945.

Fabrics old and new: Michel Biehn, 7, avenue des Quatre-Otages.

Freshly made noodles: Les Pâtes Fraîches, 12, rue Michelet.

Postcards and gifts: Galerie Archipel, 5, rue de la République.

Truffle hunter: Jean Spati, Les Souquettons, Saint-Pierre-des-Vassols, 90.62.57.72.

Wine bar: Le Caveau de la Tour d L'Isle, 12, rue de la République.

NEAR L'ISLE

CABRIÈRES D'AVIGNON, 10 km east on N100, D99, and D100. **Restaurant:** Le Bistrot à Michel (M+), 90.76.82.08.

MODÈNE, 17 km north on D938 to Carpentras,12 km east on D974, 2 km west on D55. **Restaurant:** La Table de La Truffe (M+), 90.62.35.02.

SAINT-RÉMY

Restaurants: Le Bistrot des Alpilles, 15, boulevard Mirabeau (M+), 90.92.09.17; Le Café des Arts, 30, boulevard Victor-Hugo (M+), 90.92.08.50; Le Jardin de Frédéric, 8, boulevard Gambetta (M), 90.92.27.76; La Maison Jaune, 15, rue Carnot (M+), 90.92.56.14; *Hostellerie de Vallon de Valrugues (E+), 90.92.04.40.

Basket makers: La Fabrique, 25, avenue de la Libération.

Musée des Alpilles: rue Carnot at place Favier.

Provençal dishware: Charrin, boulevard Marceau.

Van Gogh museum: l'Hotel Estrine at 8, rue Estrine.

Wholesale farmer's market: Saint-Étienne. Daily after 5 P.M. (Tuesday and Thursday in winter).

Wines of Les Baux: Domaine de Trévallon, chemin Romain d'Arles à Saint-Rémy, Saint-Étienne-du-Grès, 8.5 km east on D99; Domaine des Terres Blanches, 9 km east on D99; Mas de Gourgonnier, le Destet, 19 km southeast on D5 and D78.

NEAR SAINT-RÉMY

LES BAUX-DE-PROVENCE, 4.5 km south on D5. **Restaurants:** **Oustaù de Beaumanière (E+), 90.54.33.07;*La Riboto de Taven, Val d'Enfer (E+), 90.54.34.23.

FONTVIEILLE, 19 km south and west on D5 and D17. **Restaurant:** *La Regalido, rue Fréderic Mistral (E+) 90.54.60.22.

MAUSSANNE-LES-ALPILLES, 11 km south on D5. **Restaurant:** *La Petite France, avenue Vallée des Baux (E), 90.54.41.91. **Olive-oil cooperative:** rue Charlon-Rieu.

PARADOU, 13 km south and west on D5 and D17. **Restaurant:** Le Bistrot du Paradou (M), 90.54.32.70.

TARASCON, 16 km west on D99. **Provençal fabrics:** Souléïado, 39, rue Proudhon; the Musée Charles Deméry, same address, tours Monday through Friday by appointment, 90.91.08.80.

LA TOUR D'AIGUES

Restaurant: Auberge de la Tour (M), 90.07.34.64.

NEAR LA TOUR

LA BASTIDE-DES-JOURDANS, 11 km northeast on D956. **Restaurant:** Auberge de Cheval Blanc (M+), 90.77.81.08.

CUCURON, 13 km west on D135, D9, and D27. **Restaurants:** L'Étang (M), 90.77.21.25; L'Arbre de Mai, rue de l'Église (M), 90.77.25.10. **Olive-oil museum:** Le Vieux Moulin, rue de l'Église.

Suggested Reading

Bec, Serge. *Le Luberon et sa region.* Paris: Éditions Solars, 1992.

Brennan, Georgeanne. *Potager: Fresh Garden Cooking in the French Style.* San Francisco: Chronicle, 1992.

Christian, Glynn. *Traveler's Guide to the Food of France.* New York: Henry Holt and Co., 1986.

David, Elizabeth. *French Country Cooking,* 2d. rev. ed. Harmondsworth: Penguin Books, 1966.

Fisher, M. F. K. *Two Towns in Provence.* New York: Vintage Books, 1983.

Forbes, Leslie, ed. *A Taste of Provence: Classic Recipes from the South of France.* Boston: Little, Brown, 1987.

Jacobs, Michael. *A Guide to Provence.* Harmondsworth: Penguin, 1988.

Johnston, Mireille. *The Cuisine of the Sun: Classical French Cooking from Nice and Provence.* New York: Random House, 1979.

Mayle, Peter. *A Year in Provence.* New York: Vintage, 1989.

———. *Toujours Provence.* New York: Knopf, 1991.

More, Carey and Julian. *A Taste of Provence.* London: Pavilion Books, 1988.

Mouriès, Nathalie. *Guide Provence de Charme.* Paris: Éditions Payot et Rivages, 1995.

Ollivier-Elliot, Patrick. *Luberon: Carnets d'un voyageur attentif.* Aix-en-Provence: Edisud, 1991.

———. *Luberon: Carnets d'un voyageur attentif; Pays d'Aigues.* Aix-en-Provence: Edisud, 1993.

Olney, Richard. *Lulu's Provençal Table.* New York: HarperCollins, 1994.

Olney, Richard et al. *Provence the Beautiful Cookbook.* San Francisco: Collins, 1993.

Parker, Robert M., Jr. *The Wines of the Rhône Valley and Provence.* New York: Simon and Schuster, 1987.

Pebeyre, Pierre-Jean and Jacques. *Le grand livre de la truffe.* Paris: Daniel Briand-Robert Laffont, 1987.

Roch, Edward. *Eating Out in Provence and the Côte d'Azur.* New York: Interlink, 1992.

Spurrier, Steven. *French Country Wines.* London: Collins, 1984.

Wells, Patricia. *The Food Lover's Guide to France.* New York: Workman Publishers, 1987.

Willan, Anne, and École de la Cuisine, La Varenne, Paris. *French Regional Cooking.* New York: William Morrow, 1981.

Wylie, Laurence. *Village in the Vaucluse.* 3d ed. Cambridge, Mass., and London, England: Harvard University Press, 1974.

List of Recipes

APERITIF
Red Wine Kir 27

FIRST COURSES
Green Garlic Soup 9
Salad of Green Beans, Sausage, and Bacon 23
Mussel and Chard Soup Provençal 37
Tomatoes Provençal with Anchovy Persillade 59
Shrimp and Zucchini Fritters with Red Pepper Puree 62
Lentil Salad with Goat Cheese 84
Frisée Salad with Chicken Livers 95

MAIN COURSES
Grilled Quail with Green Onions and Tapenade Croutons 10
Ratatouille with Poached Quail Eggs 24
Stuffed Leg of Alpilles Lamb 44
Pasta with Garlic Cream and Tomatoes 94
Vegetable Soup with Pistou 108
Risotto with Marrow and Truffles 111

DESSERTS
Cherries with Sabayon Brûlé 15
Cavaillon Melons with Beaumes de Venise 28
Poached Pears with Peppercorns and Wine Sorbet 35
Carpentras Strawberries with Almond-Orange Meringue Cookies 64
Peach and Raspberry Tart 87
Lavender Honey Ice Cream with Pistachio Brittle 97
Figs with Caramel Sauce 110

Index

For a list of the recipes in this book, see page 129.

131